At Issue

Can Glacier and Ice Melt Be Reversed?

Other Books in the At Issue Series:

At Issue

Can Glacier and Ice Melt Be Reversed?

Roman Espejo, Book Editor

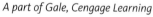

GREENHAVEN PRESS
A part of Gale, Cengage Learning

GALE
CENGAGE Learning·

Detroit • New York • San Francisco • New Haven, Conn • Waterville, Maine • London

CENGAGE Learning·

Elizabeth Des Chenes, *Director, Content Strategy*
Cynthia Sanner, *Publisher*
Douglas Dentino, Manager, *New Product*

For more information, contact:
Greenhaven Press
27500 Drake Rd.
Farmington Hills, MI 48331-3535
Or you can visit our Internet site at gale.cengage.com

For product information and technology assistance, contact us at

Gale Customer Support, 1-800-877-4253
For permission to use material from this text or product, submit all requests online at
www.cengage.com/permissions

Further permissions questions can be e-mailed to permissionrequest@cengage.com

Articles in Greenhaven Press anthologies are often edited for length to meet page require-ments. In addition, original titles of these works are changed to clearly present the main thesis and to explicitly indicate the author's opinion. Every effort is made to ensure that Greenhaven Press accurately reflects the original intent of the authors. Every effort has been made to trace the owners of copyrighted material.

Cover image © Debra Hughes 2007. Used under license from Shutterstock.com.

LIBRARY OF CONGRESS CATALOGING-IN-PUBLICATION DATA

Can glacier and ice melt be reversed? / Roman Espejo, book editor.
    pages cm. -- (At issue)
    Includes bibliographical references and index.
    ISBN 978-0-7377-6826-8 (hardcover) -- ISBN 978-0-7377-6827-5 (pbk.)
    1. Glaciers--Climatic factors--Arctic regions. 2. Glaciers--Climatic factors--Polar regions. 3. Climatic changes--Environmental aspects--Arctic regions. 4. Climatic changes--Environmental aspects--Polar regions. 5. Sea ice--Arctic regions. 6. Sea ice--Polar regions. 7. Global warming--Arctic regions. 8. Global warming--Polar regions. I. Espejo, Roman, 1977- editor of compilation.
    QC903.2.A68C36 2014
    551.31--dc23
                                                            2013037190

Printed in the United States of America
1 2 3 4 5 6 7 18 17 16 15 14

Contents

Introduction

The term cryosphere is derived from the Greek words *kryos* (cold) and *sphaira* (globe). It refers to the world's frozen places, where water exists in solid forms—ice and snow. "People most often think of the cryosphere as being at the top and bottom of our planet, in the polar regions,"[1] states the National Snow & Ice Data Center (NSIDC). "But snow and ice are also found at many other locations on Earth." This includes the high elevations of Mount Kilimanjaro in Tanzania and the Rocky Mountains in the United States. During the winter, the cryosphere grows, marked by snow cover and frozen bodies of water and soil.

The cryosphere is composed of various types of areas that differ in size, properties, and composition. Glaciers are large masses of ice formed from compressed snow. Currently, they cover 5.8 million square miles of the Earth's surface and contain 75 percent of its freshwater. Sizes range from patches the size of a football field to rivers more than 100 miles long. "In a way, glaciers are just frozen rivers of ice flowing downhill,"[2] explains the US Geological Survey (USGS). "These 'rivers' of ice are tremendously heavy, and if they are on land that has a downhill slope the whole ice patch starts to slowly grind its way downhill," adds the USGS.

Various terms are used to describe glacial formations. If the mass is dome shaped and covers a mountain, mountain range, or volcano—but less than 19,000 square miles—it is called an ice cap. But when it follows the shape of the underlying terrain and connects other glaciers, it is an ice field. When a long, narrow section of ice sticks out from the base of

1. National Snow & Ice Data Center, "All About the Cryosphere," accessed March 6, 2013. http://nsidc.org/cryosphere/allaboutcryosphere.html.
2. US Geological Survey, "Glaciers and Ice Caps: Storehouses of Freshwater," accessed March 6, 2013. http://ga.water.usgs.gov/edu/earthglacier.html.

a glacier, it is an ice tongue. And a glacier more than 19,000 square miles is called an ice sheet or continental glacier. Presently, only Antarctica and Greenland have ice sheets. Finally, a glacier or ice sheet connected to a landmass that floats on water is an ice shelf. When a part of an ice shelf or glacier breaks away, calving occurs, which produces icebergs. This takes place in Greenland and Alaska in the Northern Hemisphere and Antarctica and Chile in the Southern Hemisphere.

Frozen seawater is known as sea ice. "It forms, grows, and melts in the ocean. In contrast, icebergs, glaciers, ice sheets, and ice shelves all originate on land,"[3] maintains the NSIDC. It covers 9.7 million square miles of the Earth, found primarily in polar regions. Sea ice is distinctive from lake or river ice in several ways. Due to constantly moving waters, it takes various shapes and does not form a smooth surface. In addition, the salt in seawater affects how sea ice forms. "In contrast to fresh water, the salt in ocean water causes the density of the water to increase as it nears the freezing point, and very cold ocean water tends to sink," states the NSIDC. "As a result, sea ice forms slowly, compared to freshwater ice, because salt water sinks away from the cold surface before it cools enough to freeze."

Permafrost is soil or ground containing water that is frozen, existing where the ground remains at the freezing point (32 degrees Fahrenheit) for at least two years in a row. Found in the Arctic, Alaska, Canada, and Russia, it totals an area of nine million square miles in the Northern Hemisphere, where the majority of permafrost is located. In the Southern Hemisphere, it is found in South America, New Zealand, and Antarctica, where rare bare ground is permanently frozen. "Permafrost occurs in lower-latitude mountainous regions and plateaus of both hemispheres and is commonly referred to as mountain (or alpine) permafrost and plateau permafrost, re-

---

3. National Snow & Ice Data Center, "All About Sea Ice," accessed March 6, 2013. http://nsidc.org/cryosphere/seaice.

spectively,"[4] observe scientists J. Alan Heginbottom, Jerry Brown, Ole Humlum, and Harald Svensson. Permafrost with very little or no ice is called dry permafrost.

Lastly, snow cover makes up most of the cryosphere, blanketing 17.8 million square miles of the world each year. It is mostly found in North America, Europe, Russia, and Greenland in the Northern Hemisphere and New Zealand, South America, and Antarctica in the Southern Hemisphere. Not all cold regions experience snowfall, however, due to insufficient moisture in the atmosphere. "Even Antarctica, the coldest and iciest continent, contains a region called the Dry Valleys, where it is extremely cold, but so dry that snow never falls,"[5] claims the NSIDC.

Often referred to as the world's "thermostat," with respect to its influence on climate and weather, the cryosphere and its current state is under vigorous debate. *At Issue: Can Glacier and Ice Melt Be Reversed?* addresses the issues, from the shrinking of glaciers to the consequences of thawing permafrost. The diverse perspectives, reports, and critiques selected for this anthology represent not only the discoveries and implications of cryospheric research, but its challenges and drawbacks.

4. J. Alan Heginbottom et al., "Permafrost and Periglacial Environments," in *State of the Earth's Cryosphere at the Beginning of the 21st Century: Glaciers, Global Snow Cover, Floating Ice, and Permafrost and Periglacial Environments*, edited by Richard S. Williams Jr. and Jane G. Ferrigno, US Geological Survey, 2012. http://pubs.usgs.gov/pp/p1386a/Cryosphere_Notes.html.
5. National Snow & Ice Data Center, "All About Snow," accessed March 6, 2013. http://nsidc.org/cryosphere/snow/science/where.html.

1

The Melting of Glaciers Cannot Be Reversed

Tim Appenzeller

Tim Appenzeller is chief magazine editor of Nature, *former science editor of* National Geographic, *and a science journalist.*

The world's glaciers and ice sheets are melting at an increasing pace due to rising temperatures, and many will be gone in just a few decades. Rather than melting eventually, feedbacks—melting processes that cause more melting—speed up ice loss. In the Andes, for instance, exposed dark rock on glaciers absorbs heat from the sun and accelerates melting, as evidenced by vanishing ski areas. In Greenland, where the weather has significantly warmed, numerous glaciers are flowing out to sea at much faster rates, and its ice sheet is beginning to stir. And while Antarctica is more stable, some of the continent's glaciers are also losing ice more quickly, with potential for a major ice shelf collapse. Scientists conclude that this transformation in the world's cold places cannot be stopped.

Even in better times, the Chacaltaya ski area was no competition for Aspen. Set in a bleak valley high in the Andes mountains of Bolivia, it offered a half-mile (one kilometer) swoop downhill, a precarious ride back up on a rope tow, and coca-leaf tea for altitude headaches. At 17,250 feet (5,260 meters), after all, Chacaltaya was the highest ski area in the world. "It gave us a lot of glory," says Walter Laguna, the president of Bolivia's mountain club. "We organized South American championships—with Chile, with Argentina, with Colombia."

The glory days are over. Skiing at this improbable spot depended on a small glacier that made a passable ski run when Bolivia's wet season dusted it with snow. The glacier was already shrinking when the ski area opened in 1939. But in the past decade, it's gone into a death spiral.

By last year [2006] all that remained were three patches of gritty ice, the largest just a couple of hundred yards (200 meters) across. The rope tow traversed boulder fields. Laguna insists that skiing will go on. Perhaps the club can make artificial snow, he says; perhaps it can haul in slabs of ice to mend the glacier. But in the long run, he knows, Chacaltaya is history. "The process is irreversible. Global warming will continue."

Ice Loss Is Outstripping Global Warming

From the high mountains to the vast polar ice sheets, the world is losing its ice faster than anyone thought possible. Even scientists who had monitored Chacaltaya since 1991 thought it would hold out for a few more years. It's no surprise that glaciers are melting as emissions from cars and industry warm the climate. But lately, the ice loss has outstripped the upward creep of global temperatures.

The fate of many mountain glaciers is already sealed.

Scientists are finding that glaciers and ice sheets are surprisingly touchy. Instead of melting steadily, like an ice cube on a summer day, they are prone to feedbacks, when melting begets more melting and the ice shrinks precipitously. At Chacaltaya, for instance, the shrinking glacier exposed dark rocks, which sped up its demise by soaking up heat from the sun. Other feedbacks are shriveling bigger mountain glaciers ahead of schedule and sending polar ice sheets slipping into the ocean.

Most glaciers in the Alps could be gone by the end of the century, Glacier National Park's namesake ice by 2030. The small glaciers sprinkled through the Andes and Himalaya have a few more decades at best. And the prognosis for the massive ice sheets covering Greenland and Antarctica? No one knows, if only because the turn for the worse has been so sudden. Eric Rignot, a scientist at NASA's Jet Propulsion Laboratory who has measured a doubling in ice loss from Greenland over the past decade, says: "We see things today that five years ago would have seemed completely impossible, extravagant, exaggerated."

The fate of many mountain glaciers is already sealed. To keep skiing alive in Bolivia, Walter Laguna will need to find a bigger, higher ice field. And the millions of people in countries like Bolivia, Peru, and India who now depend on meltwater from mountain glaciers for irrigation, drinking, and hydropower could be left high and dry. Meanwhile, if global warming continues unabated, the coasts could drown. If vulnerable parts of the ice that blankets Greenland and Antarctica succumb, rising seas could flood hundreds of thousands of square miles—much of Florida, Bangladesh, the Netherlands—and displace tens of millions of people.

The temperature threshold for drastic sea-level rise is near, but many scientists think we still have time to stop short of it, by sharply cutting back consumption of climate-warming coal, oil, and gas. Few doubt, however, that another 50 years of business as usual will take us beyond a point of no return.

Ancient coral heads, white and dead, record an earlier time when the climate warmed and the seas rose. Found just inland in the Florida Keys, Bermuda, and the Bahamas, they date from roughly 130,000 years ago, before the last ice age. These corals grew just below the sea surface, and are now marooned well above it. When they flourished, sea level must have been 15 to 20 feet (five to six meters) higher—which means that much of the water now in Greenland's ice was sloshing in the oceans.

All it took to release that water was a few degrees of warming. Climate back then had a different driver: not fossil-fuel emissions but changes in Earth's tilt in space and its path around the sun, which warmed summers in the far North by three to five degrees Celsius (5° to 9°F) compared with today. At the rate the Arctic is now warming, those temperatures could be back soon—"by mid-century, no problem," says Jonathan Overpeck of the University of Arizona, who has studied the ancient climate. "There's just unbelievable warming in the Arctic. It's going much faster than anyone thought it could or would."

Anything but Leisurely

Computer models that forecast how ice sheets will react to the warming tend to predict a sluggish response—a few thousand years for them to melt, shrink, and catch up to the reality of a warmer world. If the models are right, rising seas are a distant threat.

Yet what is happening on the Greenland ice sheet is anything but leisurely. For the past 15 years, Konrad Steffen of the University of Colorado at Boulder has spent each spring monitoring the ice from a camp deep in the interior. Back again in the coastal village of Ilulissat last summer, the Swiss-born climate researcher, lean and weathered from wind and glacial glare, sits with colleagues in a waterfront hotel, waiting out fog that has grounded their helicopter. "Things are changing," he says. "We see it all over."

Offshore, flotillas of icebergs drift silvery in the half-light—tangible evidence of the change. Their voyage began nearby in a deep fjord, where a glacier called Jakobshavn Isbræ flows to the sea.

Ice seems rock hard when you crunch an ice cube or slip on a frozen puddle. But when piled in a great mass, ice oozes like slow, cold taffy. On Greenland, it flows outward from the heart of the ice sheet, a dome of ice the size of the Gulf of Mexico, and either peters out on land or follows fast-flowing ice streams all the way to the ocean. Four miles (six kilometers) wide and several thousand feet thick, Jakobshavn is an icy Amazon, disgorging more ice than any other Greenland glacier.

> Greenland lost a total of 54 cubic miles (225 cubic kilometers) of ice in 2005, more than twice as much as ten years ago—and more than some scientists were prepared to believe.

Jakobshavn is flowing ever faster. In the past decade it doubled its speed, to roughly 120 feet (37 meters) a day. By now it discharges 11 cubic miles (45 cubic kilometers) of ice each year, jamming the fjord with fresh icebergs.

The pace is picking up elsewhere around Greenland. Last year Eric Rignot reported satellite radar measurements showing that most glaciers draining the southern half of the Greenland ice sheet have accelerated, some even more dramatically than Jakobshavn. He calculated that Greenland lost a total of 54 cubic miles (225 cubic kilometers) of ice in 2005, more than twice as much as ten years ago—and more than some scientists were prepared to believe.

Two of the outlet glaciers have since slowed down. But other satellites detected a minuscule weakening of Greenland's gravity, confirming that it is shedding ice at a rate of tens of cubic miles a year. Says Waleed Abdalati, a NASA scientist who oversees research on Greenland and Antarctica, "The ice sheet is starting to stir."

Just as Jakobshavn accelerated, its tongue—the glacier's seaward end, floating on the waters of the fjord—began to shatter and retreat. Since 2000, the tongue has receded by four miles (six kilometers), adding to the clutter of icebergs in the fjord. Many of the other Greenland glaciers racing to the sea have also lost part or all of their tongues, which may explain the speedup. "Floating ice acts as a buttress," explains Abdalati. "It holds back the ice behind it, so that when it melts, it sort of uncorks the glacier."

Greenland's weather has warmed palpably. Winter temperatures at Steffen's ice camp have risen about five degrees Celsius (9°F) since 1993. In the past, researchers riding snowmobiles to outlying instrument stations could still count on firm snow as late as May; last year they got stuck in slush. For the past two years Ilulissat—well above the Arctic Circle, a place where street signs mark dogsled crossings—has had long winter thaws. "It was supposed to be minus 20 (−29°C)," says Steffen, "and instead it was raining."

There's little agreement about how much ice West Antarctica is losing each year. But the loss could grow, eventually adding five feet (two meters) or more to global sea level.

Offshore, the middle depths of the Atlantic have warmed as well, by several tenths of a degree—enough to undermine an ice tongue that is also melting from above. Eventually all of Greenland's floating ice could disintegrate. At that point the ice streams may stop accelerating. Then again, they may not, Steffen says. The weight of Greenland's ice sheet has forced its bedrock down into a vast basin, much of it below sea level. As the glaciers retreat inland, the ocean may follow, prying them off their bed in a runaway process of collapse.

Right now Greenland is no threat to beachfront property. Steven Nerem of the University of Colorado at Boulder, who monitors sea level by satellite, says the oceans have been rising an eighth of an inch (0.3 centimeter) a year. At that rate the sea would go up a foot (0.3 meters) by 2100, roughly what a United Nations panel on climate change predicted earlier this year. "But that's nothing compared to what we expect if Greenland really starts to go," Nerem says. . . .

Look at a map, and it's easy to see why the Greenland ice sheet is so vulnerable: Its southern end is no farther north than ice-free Anchorage or Stockholm. Greenland's ice is a relic of the last ice age, surviving only because it is massive enough to make its own climate. The island's brilliant, perpetually snow-covered interior reflects light and heat. Its elevation adds to the chill, and its bulk fends off warm weather systems from farther south. As the ice sheet shrinks, all these defenses will weaken.

A Disturbing Echo of Greenland

The bigger ice mass at the other end of the globe seems less fragile. Except for the Antarctic Peninsula, which juts past the Antarctic Circle, Antarctica is safely deep-frozen. Global warming may even be causing parts of the ice sheet to thicken, because warmer air ferries more moisture, leading to heavier snowfall. But around one remote Antarctic sea, scientists are picking up a disturbing echo of what is happening in Greenland.

The glaciers that flow into the Amundsen Sea carry ice from the heart of the West Antarctic ice sheet, the smaller of the southern continent's two ice masses. Like Greenland's ice, West Antarctica's rests on a bed that is largely below sea level. And its outlet glaciers too are stirring.

One of them, the Pine Island Glacier, a mammoth ice stream more than 20 miles (30 kilometers) wide and half a mile (one kilometer) thick, has sped up by a third since the 1970s. Another, Thwaites Glacier, has widened, gathering ever more ice into the seaward-flowing mass. There's little agreement about how much ice West Antarctica is losing each year.

But the loss could grow, eventually adding five feet (two meters) or more to global sea level.

That may have happened 130,000 years ago, the last time seas rose higher than today. The sheer magnitude of the rise, 15 to 20 feet (five to six meters), points to a contribution from Antarctica as well as Greenland. Then, as now, Antarctica was too cold to melt from above. The attack must have come from warmer oceans that undermined floating ice, triggering a partial collapse of the ice sheet. The stage is set for it to happen again, says Robert Thomas, a glacier expert who works with NASA.

The collapse he envisions would begin at Pine Island, which ends in a floating ice shelf nearly 40 miles (60 kilometers) long. Flying over it in a Chilean Navy plane, Thomas and his colleagues found that the shelf is thinning by tens of feet a year. That explains Pine Island's speedup, says Thomas: The thinning weakens the shelf's grip on the land to either side, releasing the brakes on the glacier.

More disturbing to Thomas is the "ice plain" just inland of the floating ice shelf—15 miles (24 kilometers) of dead-flat ice, resting lightly on deep bedrock. The ice plain is also thinning, and Thomas thinks that sometime in the next decade, it will be thin enough to float free.

Once that happens and the ocean intrudes, a chain reaction of collapse could follow. "The bed is very deep and flat for the next 150 miles (240 kilometers) inland, so an enormous fjord would be created in the ice," Thomas says. "That would put the nail in the coffin—it would go on accelerating, retreating, and drain a lot of that part of West Antarctica."

Thomas won't say how fast this gloomy scenario might unfold, and some other glaciologists dismiss it. But the prospect of a sneak attack from warming oceans is worrisome enough that scientists are planning major studies for the International Polar Year, a coordinated polar research effort over the next two years. Robert Bindschadler, a NASA glaciologist, wants to drill through the Pine Island ice shelf—1,800 feet

(550 meters) of floating ice—and lower instruments to see whether the ocean really is eroding the underside, and a British group may probe below the shelf with a robotic submarine.

Asked which of the world's great ice sheets worries him more, Greenland or Antarctica, Bindschadler just smiles and says, "Yes."

Shriveled, Pocked—or Simply Gone

In the thin air of the Andes, doubts evaporate. Here the fate of the ice is as distinct as the jagged gray peaks around the Tuni reservoir, a major water source for Bolivia's capital, La Paz, and its burgeoning slum, El Alto.

El Niños, which are striking more often as the climate warms, throw global weather out of kilter, starving the tropical Andes of snow.

Edson Ramírez, a Bolivian glacier researcher, is on his way to check gauges along the mountain streams that fill the reservoir. He stops his truck and unfurls aerial photos of the same peaks, made in 1983. Back then, they were bearded with glaciers. Today the glaciers are shriveled, pocked—or simply gone. A point-by-point comparison shows that half of them have vanished in 20 years, and the total ice area has shrunk by 30 percent.

"In 1995, when we predicted the disappearance of the glaciers, very few people believed us," Ramírez says. "We were accused of being alarmist. But now it has come to pass." Global warming apparently struck these glaciers a roundabout blow. Every month for the past 15 years Ramírez and other scientists led by Bernard Francou, a French glaciologist, have climbed glaciers around La Paz to measure the ice and collect weather data. They saw little direct effect from the slight warming of the atmosphere in recent years. What devastated the glaciers was a relentless series of El Niños—episodes of warming in the waters of the equatorial Pacific.

El Niños, which are striking more often as the climate warms, throw global weather out of kilter, starving the tropical Andes of snow. Normally the highest part of a tropical glacier gains thickness from snowfall during the wet season, making up for melting below. But in a snowless year, glaciers gain little ice. Meanwhile, melting accelerates—because of yet another feedback.

Snow normally acts as a protective sunblock for mountain glaciers. On one of Francou's study glaciers, a two-mile-long (three kilometers) cascade of ice called Zongo, the effect is easy to see. Zongo's upper slopes glitter with old snow, a legacy of the wet season six months ago. Reflecting the sun's light and heat, the snow keeps the ice underneath from melting. But the glacier's lower reaches are bare ice, a dull, dusty gray that absorbs solar heat like a dark T-shirt. By late morning, rivulets of melt are trickling down the ice.

An El Niño—three hit Bolivia in the 1990s—leaves most of the glacier snowless, gray, and vulnerable. Each time, the sun erodes many feet of ice, and the losses are never fully replaced. Since 1991 Zongo's surface has dropped 20 feet (six meters), and the glacier's snout has retreated 650 feet (200 meters) upslope, leaving a lake of silty meltwater.

Zongo is a relatively healthy glacier—massive and high, topping out above 19,000 feet (5,800 meters). Chacaltaya and the shrinking glaciers around the Tuni reservoir are smaller, lower, and more fragile. No bigger than city parks, and by far the most common kind of glacier in the Andes, they are bound for extinction in the years to come.

Spelling Real Trouble for Cities

The loss of a ski area is sadly symbolic. But the loss of the glaciers could spell real trouble for cities like La Paz, at the receiving end of the canals and power lines that lead out of the mountains.

Mountain glaciers play a vital role as water banks, storing it as ice during wet seasons and doling it out in dry months as melt. Ramírez has found that, year-round, glacier runoff supplies about a third of the water in Tuni; in the dry season the figure rises to 60 percent. In Peru, a major hydroelectric plant and a rich agricultural valley depend on the Santa River, where 40 percent of dry-season flow is glacial meltwater. The Ganges, the lifeline for northern India, is by some estimates 70 percent glacial in the summer—runoff from Himalayan ice fields.

From many people whose lives are bound up with ice—scientists, mountaineers, ordinary people who live near the glaciers—you hear a note of mourning.

The bounty continues for now; in some places, it has even increased, as the glaciers melt faster than ever. But cities and farms downstream will soon feel the pinch. Edson Ramírez expects La Paz and El Alto to face water shortages before the end of the decade, as demand grows and the glacial supply starts to dwindle.

"If you dry up the mountains, what happens to the cities below?" asks Walter Vergara, a Latin America climate-change expert at the World Bank. In the developing world, the question is often asked in anger. "Climate change wasn't caused by the poor countries like Bolivia," says Oscar Paz Rada of the Bolivian Ministry of Planning and Development, "and there is a debt owed them by the developed countries."

New dams and bigger reservoirs could keep water flowing through the dry season; wind or solar power could supplement fitful hydroelectric generators. These measures won't be cheap, and some, like dams in the earthquake-prone Andes, carry risks of their own. "But time won't wait," says Paz. "People need us to take action."

Losing Beloved Landscapes

Bernard Francou likes to show a whimsical photo of himself pedaling an ice-cream cart. It is his next career, he jokes, after the ice is gone. Francou is prone to dark humor. From many people whose lives are bound up with ice—scientists, mountaineers, ordinary people who live near the glaciers—you hear a note of mourning.

Glacier National Park in Montana is a fitting emblem for the great change sweeping the world's cold places. Dan Fagre has studied the glaciers in the park for 15 years. A scientist for the US Geological Survey, he has the numbers at his fingertips: 27 glaciers left in the park out of 150 a century ago, 90 percent of the ice volume gone. He gives the remainder another 25 years. "It will be the first time in at least 7,000 years that this landscape has not had glaciers."

As a scientist, he is fascinated to watch a planet being transformed. As a human being, he feels the loss of a beloved landscape. "When I go to some of the glaciers I know well, I come over the ridge, and I don't even have to pull out maps or photos," he says. "I can just look and go, Oh my gosh, that whole area's gone." Another icy landmark, seemingly as permanent as the mountains themselves, has vanished in the heat.

2

Glaciers Are Growing, Not Melting

Robert Felix

Robert Felix is author of Not by Fire but by Ice *and writes about climate issues at iceagenow.info.*

Claims that the world's glaciers are disappearing are false and based on flawed science. For instance, a major study cited for ice loss in the Himalayas contains weak and contradictory evidence: while it states that some glaciers are disappearing, based on a miniscule sample, it also reports that numerous glaciers are actually growing. In fact, the majority are growing and thickening in different parts of the world, from the United States to New Zealand. Also, while ice loss has been observed in the Antarctic Peninsula, ice is increasing in its interior and eastern areas, and Greenland's ice cap shows modest thickening, not catastrophic melting. The falsehoods touted by climate change advocates, not shrinking glaciers, should be feared.

"Almost all of the ice-covered regions of the Earth are melting—and seas are rising," said [former vice president and environmental activist] Al Gore in an op-ed piece in the *New York Times* on February 27 [2010].

Both parts of Gore's statement are false.

Never mind that Mr. Gore makes only passing reference to the IPCC [Intergovernmental Panel on Climate Change]'s fraudulent claims that the Himalayan glaciers will all melt by 2035. ("A flawed overestimate," he explains.)

Never mind that Mr. Gore dismisses the IPCC's fraudulent claims that the oceans are rising precipitously. ("Partly inaccurate," he huffs.)

Never mind that Mr. Gore completely ignores the admission by the CRU's [Climatic Research Unit] disgraced former director Phil Jones that global temperatures have essentially remained unchanged for the past 15 years.

I'll let someone else dissect Gore's lawyering comments, and concentrate on just the one sentence about melting ice, because neither part of that sentence is true.

No matter how assiduously Mr. Gore tries to ignore it, almost all of the ice-covered regions of the Earth are now gaining mass.

Growing, Not Melting

Contrary to Gore's assertions, almost all of the ice-covered regions of the Earth are *growing*, not melting—and the seas are not rising.

Let's look at the facts.

If you click on the words "are melting" in Gore's article, you're taken to a paper by Michael Zemp at the University of Zurich. Mr. Zemp begins his paper by warning that "glaciers around the globe continue to melt at high rates."

However, if you bother to actually read the paper, you learn that Zemp's conclusion is based on measurements of "more than 80 glaciers."

Considering that the Himalayas boast more than 15,000 glaciers, a study of "more than 80 glaciers" hardly seems sufficient to warrant such a catastrophic pronouncement.

Especially when you learn that of those 80 glaciers, several are growing.

Growing. Not melting.

"In Norway, many maritime glaciers were able to gain mass," Zemp concedes. ("Able to gain mass" means growing.)

In North America, Zemp also concedes, "some positive values were reported from the North Cascade Mountains and the Juneau Ice Field." ("Displaying positive values" means growing.)

Remember, we're still coming out of the last ice age. Ice is *supposed* to melt as we come out of an ice age. The ice has been melting for 11,000 years. Why should today be any different? I'm guessing that most Canadians and Northern Europeans are very happy that the ice has been melting.

Unfortunately, that millenniums-long melting trend now appears to be changing. No matter how assiduously Mr. Gore tries to ignore it, almost all of the ice-covered regions of the Earth are now *gaining* mass. (Or, displaying positive values, if you will.)

The Himalayan Glaciers

For starters, let's look at those Himalayan glaciers. In a great article, entitled "World misled over Himalayan glacier meltdown," [environmental editor of the *Sunday Times* Jonathan Leake and [reporter] Chris Hastings show that the IPCC's fraudulent claims were based on "speculation" and "not supported by any formal research."

As a matter of fact, many Himalayan glaciers are growing. In a defiant act of political incorrectness, some 230 glaciers in the western Himalayas—including Mount Everest, K2 and Nanga Parbat—are actually growing.

"These are the biggest mid-latitude glaciers in the world," says John Shroder of the University of Nebraska-Omaha. "And all of them are either holding still, or advancing."

And get this. Eighty seven of the glaciers have surged forward since the 1960s.

So much for Mr. Gore's "more than 80 glaciers."

(I don't know how many Himalayan glaciers are being monitored, but my guess would be fewer than a thousand, so it's possible that hundreds more are growing. There aren't enough glaciologists in the world to monitor them all.)

Growing Glaciers in the United States

But we don't need to look to the Himalayas for growing glaciers. Glaciers are growing in the United States.

Yes, glaciers are growing in the United States.

Look at Washington State. The Nisqually Glacier on Mt. Rainier is growing. The Emmons Glacier on Mt. Rainier is growing. Glaciers on Glacier Peak in northern Washington are growing. And Crater Glacier on Mt. Saint Helens is now larger than it was before the 1980 eruption. (I don't think all of the glaciers in Washington or Alaska are being monitored either.)

Or look at California. All seven glaciers on California's Mount Shasta are growing. This includes three-mile-long Whitney glacier, the state's largest. Three of Mount Shasta's glaciers have doubled in size since 1950.

Or look at Alaska. Glaciers are growing in Alaska for the first time in 250 years. In May of last year, [Alaska's] Hubbard Glacier was advancing at the rate of seven feet (two meters) per day—more than half-a-mile per year. And in Icy Bay, at least three glaciers advanced a third of a mile (one half kilometer) in one year.

Oh, by the way. The Juneau Icefield, with its "positive values," covers 1,505 square miles (3,900 sq km) and is the fifth-largest ice field in the Western Hemisphere. Rather interesting to know that Gore's own source admits that the fifth-largest ice field in the Western Hemisphere is growing, don't you think?

But this mere handful of growing glaciers is just an anomaly, the erstwhile Mr. Gore would have you believe.

Well, let's look at a few other countries.

- Perito Moreno Glacier, the largest glacier in Argentina, is growing.

- Pio XI Glacier, the largest glacier in Chile, is growing.

- Glaciers are growing on Mt. Logan, the tallest mountain in Canada.

- Glaciers are growing on Mt. Blanc, the tallest mountain in France.

- Glaciers are growing in Norway, says the Norwegian Water Resources and Energy Directorate (NVE).

- And the last time I checked, all 50 glaciers in New Zealand were growing.

Sea ice losses in west Antarctica over the past 30 years have been more than offset by increases in the Ross Sea region, just one sector of east Antarctica.

The Atlantic and Greenland Ice Sheets

But this is nothing. These glaciers are babies when you look at our planet's largest ice masses, namely, the Antarctic and Greenland ice sheets.

Contrary to what you may have heard, both of those huge ice sheets are growing.

In 2007, Antarctica set a new record for most ice extent since 1979, says meteorologist Joe D'Aleo. While the Antarctic Peninsula area has warmed in recent years, and ice near it diminished during the summer, the interior of Antarctica has been colder and the ice extent greater.

Antarctic sea ice is also increasing. According to Australian Antarctic Division glaciology program head Ian Allison, sea ice losses in west Antarctica over the past 30 years have been more than offset by increases in the Ross Sea region, just one sector of east Antarctica.

The Antarctic Peninsula, where the ice has been melting, is only about 1/50th the size of east Antarctica, where the ice has been growing. Saying that all of Antarctica is melting is like looking at the climate of Oregon and saying that this applies to the entire United States.

There was not any evidence of significant change in the mass of ice shelves in east Antarctica nor any indication that its ice cap was melting, says Dr. Allison. "The only significant calvings in Antarctica have been in the west." And he cautioned that calvings of the magnitude seen recently in west Antarctica might not be unusual.

"A paper to be published soon by the British Antarctic Survey in the journal *Geophysical Research Letters* is expected to confirm that over the past 30 years, the area of sea ice around the continent has expanded."

What about Greenland?

Greenland's ice-cap has thickened slightly in recent years despite wide predictions of a thaw triggered by global warming, said a team of scientists in October 2005.

The 3,000-meter (9,842-feet) thick ice-cap is a key concern in debates about climate change because a total melt would raise world sea levels by about 7 meters.

But satellite measurements show that more snow is falling and thickening the ice-cap, especially at high altitudes, according to the report in the journal *Science*.

The overall ice thickness changes are approximately plus 5 cm (1.9 inches) per year or 54 cm (21.26 inches) over 11 years, according to the experts at Norwegian, Russian and U.S. institutes led by Ola Johannessen at the Mohn Sverdrup Center for Global Ocean Studies and Operational Oceanography in Norway.

Not overwhelming growth, certainly, but a far cry from the catastrophic melting that we've been lead to believe.

More than 90 percent of the world's glaciers are growing, in other words, and all we hear about are the ones that are shrinking.

Think about that.

The Antarctic Ice Sheet is almost twice as big as the contiguous United States.

Put the Antarctic and Greenland Ice Sheets together, and they're one hundred times bigger than all of the rest of the world's glaciers combined.

More than 90 percent of the world's glaciers are growing, in other words, and all we hear about are the ones that are shrinking.

Sea Levels Remain the Same

But if so many of the world's glaciers are growing, how can sea levels remain the same?

They can't. The sea level models are wrong.

During the last ice age, sea levels stood some 370 feet (100 meters) lower than today. That's where all of the moisture came from to create those two-mile-high sheets of ice that covered so much of the north.

And just as the ice has been melting for 11,000 years, so too were sea levels rising during those same years.

But the rising has stopped.

Forget those IPCC claims. Sea levels are not rising, says Dr. Nils-Axel Mörner, one-time expert reviewer for the IPCC.

Dr. Mörner, who received his PhD in geology in 1969, is one of the greatest—if not the greatest—sea level experts in the world today. He has worked with sea level problems for 40 years in areas scattered all over the globe.

"There is no change," says Möorner. "Sea level is not changing in any way."

"There is absolutely no sea-level rise in Tuvalo," Möorner insists. "There is no change here, and there is zero sea-level rise in Bangladesh. If anything, sea levels have lowered in Bangladesh."

"We do not need to fear sea-level rise," says Mörner. "(But) we should have a fear of those people who fooled us."

So there you have it. More falsehoods from Al Gore, the multimillionaire businessman who some say is set to become the world's first carbon billionaire.

Our glaciers are *growing*, not melting—and the seas are not rising.

I agree with Dr. Mörner, but I'd make it a tad stronger. We should have a fear of those people who have conned us.

3

Third-World Stove Soot Is Target in Climate Fight

Elisabeth Rosenthal

Elisabeth Rosenthal is an international environmental reporter for The New York Times.

Soot, or black carbon, produced by primitive cookstoves in developing countries accounts for 18 percent of global warming. Its particles travel through and warm the air, collect on glaciers, and absorb heat, causing them to shrink. Reducing this source of emissions offers a simple and effective solution to decreasing ice melt. It can be achieved by replacing wood and dung-burning cookstoves with modern or cleaner-burning ones, and the impact would be immediate as black carbon remains in the atmosphere for only several weeks. However, this strategy faces several obstacles, such as the affordability of new appliances, villagers' resistance to losing the taste of traditional foods, and durability of alternative cookstoves.

"It's hard to believe that this is what's melting the glaciers," said Dr. Veerabhadran Ramanathan, one of the world's leading climate scientists, as he weaved through a warren of mud brick huts, each containing a mud cookstove pouring soot into the atmosphere.

As women in ragged saris of a thousand hues bake bread and stew lentils in the early evening over fires fueled by twigs and dung, children cough from the dense smoke that fills their homes. Black grime coats the undersides of thatched roofs. At dawn, a brown cloud stretches over the landscape like a diaphanous dirty blanket.

In Kohlua, in central India, with no cars and little electricity, emissions of carbon dioxide, the main heat-trapping gas linked to global warming, are near zero. But soot—also known as black carbon—from tens of thousands of villages like this one in developing countries is emerging as a major and previously unappreciated source of global climate change.

While carbon dioxide maybe the No. 1 contributor to rising global temperatures, scientists say, black carbon has emerged as an important No. 2, with recent studies estimating that it is responsible for 18 percent of the planet's warming, compared with 40 percent for carbon dioxide. Decreasing black carbon emissions would be a relatively cheap way to significantly rein in global warming—especially in the short term, climate experts say. Replacing primitive cooking stoves with modern versions that emit far less soot could provide a much-needed stopgap, while nations struggle with the more difficult task of enacting programs and developing technologies to curb carbon dioxide emissions from fossil fuels.

Converting to low-soot cookstoves would remove the warming effects of black carbon quickly, while shutting a coal plant takes years to substantially reduce global CO2 concentrations.

In fact, reducing black carbon is one of a number of relatively quick and simple climate fixes using existing technologies—often called "low hanging fruit"—that scientists say should be plucked immediately to avert the worst projected consequences of global warming. "It is clear to any person who cares about climate change that this will have a huge impact on the global environment," said Dr. Ramanathan, a professor of climate science at the Scripps Institute of Oceanography, who is working with the Energy and Resources Institute in New Delhi on a project to help poor families acquire new stoves.

"In terms of climate change we're driving fast toward a cliff, and this could buy us time," said Dr. Ramanathan, who left India 40 years ago but returned to his native land for the project.

Better still, decreasing soot could have a rapid effect. Unlike carbon dioxide, which lingers in the atmosphere for years, soot stays there for a few weeks. Converting to low-soot cookstoves would remove the warming effects of black carbon quickly, while shutting a coal plant takes years to substantially reduce global CO2 concentrations.

But the awareness of black carbon's role in climate change has come so recently that it was not even mentioned as a warming agent in the 2007 summary report by the Intergovernmental Panel on Climate Change that pronounced the evidence for global warming to be "unequivocal." Mark Z. Jacobson, professor of environmental engineering at Stanford, said that the fact that black carbon was not included in international climate efforts was "bizarre," but "partly reflects how new the idea is." The United Nations is trying to figure out how to include black carbon in climate change programs, as is the federal government.

In Asia and Africa, cookstoves produce the bulk of black carbon, although it also emanates from diesel engines and coal plants there. In the United States and Europe, black carbon emissions have already been reduced significantly by filters and scrubbers.

Like tiny heat-absorbing black sweaters, soot particles warm the air and melt the ice by absorbing the sun's heat when they settle on glaciers. One recent study estimated that black carbon might account for as much as half of Arctic warming. While the particles tend to settle overtime and do not have the global reach of greenhouse gases, they do travel, scientists now realize. Soot from India has been found in the Maldive Islands and on the Tibetan Plateau; from the United States, it travels to the Arctic. The environmental and geopolitical implications of soot emissions are enormous. Himalayan glaciers are expected to lose 75 percent of their ice by 2020, according to Prof. Syed Iqbal Hasnain, a glacier specialist from the Indian state of Sikkim.

These glaciers are the source of most of the major rivers in Asia. The short-term result of glacial melt is severe flooding in mountain communities. The number of floods from glacial lakes is already rising sharply, Professor Hasnain said. Once the glaciers shrink, Asia's big rivers will run low or dry for part of the year, and desperate battles over water are certain to ensue in a region already rife with conflict.

Doctors have long railed against black carbon for its devastating health effects in poor countries. The combination of health and environmental benefits means that reducing soot provides a "very big bang for your buck," said Erika Rosenthal, a senior lawyer at Earth Justice, a Washington organization. "Now it's in everybody's self-interest to deal with things like cookstoves—not just because hundreds of thousands of women and children far away are dying prematurely."

In the United States, black carbon emissions are indirectly monitored and minimized through federal and state programs that limit small particulate emissions, a category of particles damaging to human health that includes black carbon. But in March, a bill was introduced in Congress that would require the Environmental Protection Agency to specifically regulate black carbon and direct aid to black carbon reduction projects abroad, including introducing cookstoves in 20 million homes. The new stoves cost about $20 and use solar power or are more efficient. Soot is reduced by more than 90 percent. The solar stoves do not use wood or dung. Other new stoves simply burn fuel more cleanly, generally by pulverizing the fuel first and adding a small fan that improves combustion.

Replacing hundreds of millions of cookstoves—the source of heat, food and sterile water—is not a simple matter.

That remote rural villages like Kohlua could play an integral role in tackling the warming crisis is hard to imagine. There are no cars—the village chief's ancient white Jeep sits highly polished but unused in front of his house, a museum piece. There is no running water and only intermittent electricity, which powers a few light bulbs.

The 1,500 residents here grow wheat, mustard and potatoes and work as day laborers in Agra, home of the Taj Majal, about two hours away by bus.

They earn about $2 a day and, for the most part, have not heard about climate change. But they have noticed frequent droughts in recent years that scientists say may be linked to global warming. Crops ripen earlier and rot more frequently than they did 10 years ago. The villagers are aware, too, that black carbon can corrode. In Agra, cookstoves and diesel engines are forbidden in the area around the Taj Majal, because soot damages the precious facade.

Still, replacing hundreds of millions of cookstoves—the source of heat, food and sterile water—is not a simple matter. "I'm sure they'd look nice, but I'd have to see them, to try them," said Chetram Jatrav, as she squatted by her cookstove making tea and a flatbread called roti. Her three children were coughing.

She would like a stove that "made less smoke and used less fuel" but cannot afford one, she said, pushing a dung cake bought for one rupee into the fire. She had just bought her first rolling pin so her flatbread could come out "nice and round," as her children had seen in elementary school. Equally important, the open fires of cookstoves give some of the traditional foods their taste. Urging these villagers to make roti in a solar cooker meets the same mix of rational and irrational resistance as telling an Italian that risotto tastes just fine if cooked in the microwave.

In March, the cookstove project, called Surya, began "market testing" six alternative cookers in villages, in part to quantify their benefits. Already, the researchers fret that the new stoves look like scientific instruments and are fragile; one broke when a villager pushed twigs in too hard.

But if black carbon is ever to be addressed on a large scale, acceptance of the new stoves is crucial. "I'm not going to go to the villagers and say CO_2 is rising, and in 50 years you might have floods," said Dr. Ibrahim Rehman, Dr. Ramanathan's collaborator at the Energy and Resources Institute. "I'll tell her about the lungs and her kids and I know it will help with climate change as well."

4

The Melting of Arctic Ice Cannot Be Reversed

Fen Montaigne

Fen Montaigne is senior editor of Yale Environment 360 *and author of* Fraser's Penguins: A Journey to the Future in Antarctica. *The following article was originally published at* Yale Environment 360. *http://e360.yale.edu/feature/tipping_point _arctic_heads_to_ice_free_summers/2567.*

The Arctic has reached record lows in sea ice extent and sea ice volume. Scientists propose that these milestones are proof that the region has reached a tipping point for ice loss and, in the next decade, will virtually be ice-free during the summer season. Factors driving the cycle of dramatic melting are the expansion of heat-absorbing dark waters due to thinning ice, warm air eliminating ice in the Arctic basin and breaking apart the ice pack, and rising levels of carbon dioxide warming the region and the globe. It is conceivable that Arctic sea ice could return if atmospheric and weather patterns change, but data collected with the newest technology indicate that a reversal of ice loss is highly unlikely.

As the northern summer draws to a close, two milestones have been reached in the Arctic Ocean—record-low sea ice extent, and an even more dramatic new low in Arctic sea ice volume. This extreme melting offers dramatic evidence, many scientists say, that the region's sea ice has passed a tipping point and that sometime in the next decade or two the North Pole will be largely ice-free in summer.

NASA and U.S. ice experts announced earlier this week [in August 2012] that the extent of Arctic sea ice has dropped to 4.1 million square kilometers (1.58 million square miles)—breaking the previous record set in 2007—and will likely continue to fall even farther until mid-September. As the summer melt season ends, the Arctic Ocean will be covered with 45 percent less ice than the average from 1979 to 2000.

Even more striking is the precipitous decline in the volume of ice in the Arctic Ocean. An analysis conducted by the University of Washington's Pan Arctic Ice Ocean Model Assimilation System (PIOMAS) estimates that sea ice volumes fell in late August to roughly 3,500 cubic kilometers—a 72-percent drop from the 1979–2010 mean.

Peter Wadhams, who heads the Polar Ocean Physics Group at the University of Cambridge and who has been measuring Arctic Ocean ice thickness from British Navy submarines, says that earlier calculations about Arctic sea ice loss have grossly underestimated how rapidly the ice is disappearing. He believes that the Arctic is likely to become ice-free before 2020 and possibly as early as 2015 or 2016—decades ahead of projections made just a few years ago.

Mark Drinkwater, mission scientist for the European Space Agency's CryoSat satellite and the agency's senior advisor on polar regions, said he and his colleagues have been taken aback by the swiftness of Arctic sea ice retreat in the last 5 years. "If this rate of melting [in 2012] is sustained in 2013, we are staring down the barrel and looking at a summer Arctic which is potentially free of sea ice within this decade," Drinkwater said in an e-mail interview.

A Point of No Return

A small number of climate scientists say that natural variability may be playing a significant role in the rapid retreat of

Arctic sea ice, intensifying human-caused climate change, and they caution against predicting the imminent demise of the region's summer sea ice. But an overwhelming majority of Arctic ice experts say that recent data offer powerful evidence that summer sea ice has passed a point of no return.

Steadily rising levels of carbon dioxide being pumped into the atmosphere by human activity are continuing to warm the Arctic and the rest of the globe, further hastening the loss of Arctic Ocean ice.

The dramatic ice loss is being driven by several key factors, scientists say. Chief among them is that decades of warming have so extensively melted and thinned Arctic sea ice that rapidly expanding areas of dark, open water are absorbing ever-greater amounts of the sun's radiation, further warming the region in a vicious cycle.

Second, swiftly warming air and ocean temperatures in the Arctic have, for now at least, altered atmospheric activity, with two consequences: Warmer air is being pulled into the Arctic, and increased storms and cyclones in summer are not only driving ice out of the Arctic basin, but also breaking up the ice pack and further exposing more dark water.

And finally there is the inescapable reality that steadily rising levels of carbon dioxide being pumped into the atmosphere by human activity are continuing to warm the Arctic and the rest of the globe, further hastening the loss of Arctic Ocean ice. Several experts say that the only thing that could slow this disappearance—and then only for a few years—would be a major volcanic eruption that reduces the amount of the sun's energy striking the earth.

"It's sobering to see the Arctic change so rapidly," said Ted Scambos, senior research scientist at the National Snow & Ice Data Center in Colorado. "Simply staring at the satellite data that we're seeing every day is awesome, but in a sad sort of way. It doesn't look like the Arctic anymore. The summer ice used to look like a cap that nearly filled the Arctic basin. It now looks like a raft with room on every side. You can imagine what it's going to look like when the North Pole is open water, when there is only a tiny amount of ice left in August and September. The planet will look a lot different."

Profound Effects

The loss of the great white dome of ice at the top of the world in summer will have profound effects, scientists say. These include a reduction of the amount of solar radiation reflected back into space by the ice, significant changes to the jet stream and Northern Hemispheric weather patterns, and even more rapid warming in the far north, speeding the melting of Greenland's massive ice sheets and increasing global sea levels.

In addition to these impacts, said Drinkwater, "Increased storminess will generate ocean wave systems which, undamped by the presence of sea ice, will pound the circumpolar north coastlines. Current rates of coastal permafrost degradation will be accelerated, leading to significant coastal erosion and reconfiguration of the high-latitude shoreline. Meanwhile, we have also recently heard about the potential for release of sub-sea methane deposits and thereby an acceleration of the current greenhouse effect."

The record low sea ice extent in 2007 of 4.2 million square kilometers was due to some unusual circumstances, including a sunny summer in the Arctic and higher temperatures. Summer sea ice extent rebounded somewhat in the next several years, rising to 5.3 million square kilometers in 2009, giving some hope to mainstream scientists that Arctic sea ice was not in a "death spiral."

But Scambos and other experts say that recent data on plummeting ice extent and volume show that the Arctic has entered a "new normal" in which ice decline seems irreversible. Because of thinning ice and swiftly expanding areas of open water, the Arctic Ocean will no longer be kept frigid in summer by the reflectivity of snow and ice—the so-called ice-albedo effect, in which ice and snow reflect a high percentage of the sun's energy back into space.

The Arctic's Higher Sensitivity

Thick sea ice that formed over many years is increasingly rare in the Arctic. In the 1960s, submarines routinely encountered 12-foot-thick ice around the North Pole and 20-foot-thick ice in some other areas; now those regions often contain ice that is only three to four feet thick. Many parts of the Arctic Ocean are now covered with thin, year-old ice that melts quickly in spring and summer.

Changing weather patterns, related to more heat and moisture being released into the Arctic atmosphere, have played a significant role in accelerating sea ice loss.

This spring, noted Scambos, extensive late winter snow cover on land melted unusually rapidly, reaching record low levels by June. Sea ice across much of the Arctic began to melt 10 to 14 days earlier than in the preceding few decades. Relatively clear skies from late May through June further hastened the melting of sea ice, but even as cloudier weather prevailed in July and August, the record sea ice retreat continued.

"The sensitivity of the Arctic to a warm summer is much higher now than it was in the 1990s or early 2000s," said Scambos. "What we're seeing last year and this year is that 2007 wasn't a fluke. As we've gone forward a few years, we're seeing that many different patterns of weather lead to significant sea ice loss in the Arctic."

Scambos does not foresee summer sea ice in the Arctic largely disappearing this decade, estimating that such an event could occur around 2030, "plus or minus a decade." He said the "endgame" of Arctic summer sea ice will probably mean that around 1 million square kilometers—about 15 percent of what existed in the mid-20th century—will remain in the Canadian High Arctic and some other regions, leaving the North Pole generally ice-free in August and September.

Drinkwater said that changing weather patterns, related to more heat and moisture being released into the Arctic atmosphere, have played a significant role in accelerating sea ice loss. Sea ice retreat in the past decade has been accompanied by a trend toward lower atmospheric pressure and more storms and cyclonic activity, which in turn breaks up the pack ice and exposes more open water. A powerful Arctic storm earlier this month did just that, Drinkwater noted.

He said that Arctic sea ice could conceivably rebound for some period of time if atmospheric circulation changes and a pattern known as the Arctic Oscillation—currently in a positive phase—moves into a negative phase and ushers in a period of prolonged high atmospheric pressure and fewer storms. This, said Drinkwater, would enable sea ice to remain trapped in the Arctic basin and thicken.

"However," added Drinkwater, "this seems like blind hope in a system whose feedbacks all appear geared to getting rid of sea ice."

Judith Curry, a climatologist and chair of the School of Earth and Atmospheric Sciences at the Georgia Institute of Technology, said that while global warming is "almost certainly" affecting Arctic sea ice, she cautioned that there is a great deal of annual and decadal variability in sea ice cover. She said that the next 5 to 10 years could see a shift in Arctic sea ice behavior, though exactly in which direction is difficult to predict.

"I don't see [the] summer of 2012 portending some sort of near-term 'spiral of death' in the sea ice behavior," Curry said in an e-mail interview. "I don't think this apparent record sea ice minimum is of particular significance in our understanding of climate variability and change of Arctic sea ice."

Little Likelihood of a Reversal

Jay Zwally, chief cryospheric scientist at NASA's Goddard Space Flight Center and an observer of Arctic ice for 40 years, places little stock in the likelihood of a reversal of disappearing Arctic ice. New satellite technology has given scientists the ability to measure the height of sea ice above the water, and hence ice volume. Those measurements, he said, have vividly underscored that Arctic sea ice is in a swoon.

For example, a recent analysis of data from CryoSat and NASA's ICESat satellite estimates that the volume of sea ice in a large area of the central Arctic Ocean has plummeted in late winter—February and March—by nearly half in just eight years, from an estimated 13,000 cubic kilometers in 2004 to 7,000 cubic kilometers in 2012.

"We've gone through a tipping point, and of all the things a tipping point applies to, sea ice is the most appropriate, because the idea is when it goes below a certain thickness it doesn't go back under present conditions," said Zwally. "People can get hung up on the specifics and lose track of the big picture, which is that it's getting worse and it's going to get [even] worse."

5

The Media Exaggerates the Extent of Ice Melt in the Arctic

Ben Pile

Based in Oxford, England, Ben Pile is convenor of the Oxford Salon and lead blogger at Climate Resistance.

Citing research on "unprecedented" Arctic ice melt, journalists and policy makers portray a battle between infallible scientists and climate-change skeptics. This represents a flawed understanding of the data, resulting from the media's tendency to take studies out of context and turn findings on Greenland's ice sheet into alarmist headlines and political statements. Various experts point out that the area's ice is not vanishing and observations of such losses, in a scientific framework, are actually expected. Even some researchers, however, have a hand in perpetuating dramatic stories about climate change and peddle sensationalism to the press. As long as science is continually upheld as unequivocal and uncorrupted, changes recorded in the earth's polar regions will be exaggerated.

'Satellites see Unprecedented Greenland Ice Sheet Melt', announced a press release on 24 July [2012] from the NASA Jet Propulsion Laboratory at the California Institution of Technology. Satellites that constantly scan environmental conditions on the planet's surface had revealed that from 8 July to 12 July, 97 per cent of the surface of the ice sheet contained water rather than ice, whereas typically just 45 per cent of the surface area melts at this time of year. The extent of this melt is not in itself significant—just millimetres on top of an ice sheet that is 3.5 kilometres thick at its deepest point, most of which soon refreezes.

In spite of the headline, the press release itself went on to explain how the 'unprecedented' extent of surface ice melt wasn't, in fact, unprecedented. 'Ice cores from Summit [a central Greenland station] show that melting events of this type occur about once every 150 years on average. With the last one happening in 1889, this event is right on time', said Lora Koenig, a NASA researcher involved in the analysis of the satellite data.

In plain sight of the fact that the melting was neither unexpected nor unprecedented, environmental journalists the world over picked up the story and ran with it. In the *Guardian*, Suzanne Goldenberg, wrote: 'The Greenland ice sheet melted at a faster rate this month than at any other time in recorded history, with virtually the entire ice sheet showing signs of thaw.'

As I have noted elsewhere, *Guardian* journalists have a fetish for stories about melting ice. In September last year, following an unusually low measurement of Arctic sea-ice extent, Damian Carrington wrote: 'Ice is the white flag being waved by our planet, under fire from the atmospheric attack being mounted by humanity.' But the low measurement of sea ice that Carrington pointed to disagreed with at least five other continuous measurements of the Arctic, and was thus unreliable. This kind of overreaction to scientific developments is a facile attempt to turn science into stories of political intrigue. When images of the Arctic taken by US spy satellites were declassified in 2009, the headline of an article by Goldenberg and Carrington proclaimed that 'the secret evidence of global warming Bush tried to hide' had been 'revealed'.

Corrections Have Limited Potential

The rash of excited articles about the dying cryosphere caused some surprising corrective responses from voices within climate research. Malte Humpert from the Arctic Institute Centre wrote a stinging response to the headline histrionics. 'The Greenland ice sheet, which is up to 3000+ metres thick, is not "melting away", did not "melt in four days", it is not "melting fast", and Greenland did not "lose 97 per cent of its surface ice layer".' Humpert continued: 'Most articles also exaggerated the importance of the melt event on global sea levels by explaining how sea levels would rise by up to 7.2 metres if the ice sheet were to melt.'

Far from being scientific, prognosticating about the future of the world on the basis of the progress of ice is like reading frog entrails.

Similarly, Mark Brandon, a sea-ice scientist at the Open University, reproduced an interesting series of tweets and links to articles that showed the development of the current panic about ice, beginning with (alleged) comedian Marcus Brigstocke's misconception of the story. To Brigstocke, an 'unprecedented' melt was the proverbial canary in the coal mine—a harbinger of doom. But as Brandon and his colleagues pointed out, it was a bit soon to be calling time on the human race. This was just weather.

Although it is good to see scientists engaging critically with climate alarmism, such corrections seem to have limited potential. Although climate activists and politicians have emphasised the scientific consensus on climate change, their alarmism has found its expression in the public sphere after press releases announcing scientific claims. These press-released stories often turn out to be based not on research, but on opinion or guesswork. For instance, in 2007, when Arctic sea ice reached its lowest extent since 1979, a rash of speculation followed about when the ice might disappear altogether. In 2008, the *Observer* happily reported that 2013 would be the date of the ice cap's demise, according to just one researcher's claim.

But this turned out to be mere guesswork, as did other estimates of the future of Arctic sea ice, which put the date of disappearance much further into the future. The fact of this speculation was lost by journalists emphasising the scientific credentials of those doing the guessing; it was guesswork, but it was *scientists'* guesswork.

Far from Scientific

Science has not put a stop to climate alarmism. The dynamics of the most barren and lifeless parts of the planet have become the ground on which the climate wars have been fought. And each 'unprecedented' move of any glacier, iceberg or sea ice becomes a moment of significance, seemingly telling us our future. Far from being scientific, prognosticating about the future of the world on the basis of the progress of ice is like reading frog entrails.

> *Endless stories about glaciers melting, polar bears, ice sheets in Greenland and Antarctica and sea ice form the view that there is virtually no ice left on the surface of the planet.*

So what has science got to say about such fortune-telling, and what can it achieve? I asked Mark Brandon about what had moved him to write his corrective of the stories that followed NASA's press release. 'When I talk to people who don't really know about polar science, they look at that picture of Greenland covered in red, and they think the whole ice sheet is melting', says Brandon. 'This isn't a story about sea-level rise. But that is how virtually everyone has presented it. And that is how almost everyone has interpreted it as well.'

Brandon is keen to emphasise that this doesn't mean that Arctic ice is not melting or that such melting is not a problem. Rather, he argues that overstating the problem is not helpful. 'I don't think many of these stories make much sense in isolation. . . . If you view things in isolation then geographically it doesn't make any sense. It doesn't make any sense from a climate point of view, which is what I [and other scientists] were trying to say. That's not to say I don't think it's melting. I think it is. But it's going for the headline. It's an easy media thing. It's a weather event. The temperature [in Greenland] only reached over zero for a few days. It would be the equivalent of a weather event going over Britain.'

If Brandon's caution reflects the consensus position on climate science, it seems to be out-of-kilter with the wider public discussion about the climate. Endless stories about glaciers melting, polar bears, ice sheets in Greenland and Antarctica and sea ice form the view that there is virtually no ice left on the surface of the planet. And there is no doubting the influence of such alarmism. Just prior to the 2009 COP15 [Conference of the Parties] climate summit in Copenhagen, then UK prime minister Gordon Brown told the world: 'We should never allow ourselves to lose sight of the catastrophe we face if present warming trends continue. Only last week, we saw new evidence of the rapid loss of Arctic sea ice. . . . And in just twenty-five years, the glaciers in the Himalayas which provide water for three-quarters of a billion people could disappear entirely. . . . And the recent report of the Global Humanitarian Forum led by Kofi Annan suggests that . . . effects of climate change are already killing 300,000 people . . . and the total will rise to half a million each year by 2030'.

What was striking about Brown's claims is that they owed nothing to science at all, let alone to the scientific consensus. Instead, the claims had come from the Caitlin mission to the Arctic—a PR [public relations] and media stunt designed to highlight the shrinking of the Arctic—and from the Global

Humanitarian Forum's [GHF] crude estimate of the effects of climate on poorer parts of the world that had emphasised climate, rather than lack of wealth, as the fundamental in the condition of the world's poor.

Ironically, the deep cold of the Arctic caused the Caitlin's equipment to fail, and ultimately the hostile weather meant the team had to be rescued. The Global Humanitarian Forum folded before the World Health Organisation's recent announcement that incidences of malaria—one of the diseases the GHF predicted would increase with global warming—had fallen dramatically since 2000.

Illiteracy Afflicts Journalists and Scientists

What most frustrates climate sceptics is the persistence of such junk science in the public and policy debates. Those who point out the problems of making arguments for policy on the back of PR stunts and junk science are labelled as 'sceptics' or 'deniers', motivated by profit, 'ideology' or simple bad-mindedness rather than the desire for a sensible debate about our relationship with the natural environment and concern about development. Brown's errors are passed over with little criticism from science. But how to account for such errors in the first place?

One problem, says Brandon, is that a clear view of science is precluded by the expectations weighing on scientists, who may be reluctant to enter a fierce debate. He imagines a case of a researcher producing work that explained where climate models are going wrong: 'If he or she stood up and talked to a journalist, that very good research intended to improve the models could have her work framed as saying that climate models are garbage, therefore the Arctic isn't warming.' In other words, in a highly polarised debate, scientific developments are taken to be decisive. Mistakes in computer models are taken to be the final word on the paucity of evidence of manmade climate change, and an anomalous measurement of Greenland's ice sheet spells the end of the world.

Another problem is that journalists and policymakers simply do not understand the context of research. Brandon compares a lay reading of climate science to an attempt to read a Jane Austen novel at face value. Without historical knowledge of the grammatical nuances and peculiarities of eighteenth- and nineteenth-century society, the significance of events in Austen's plots may be lost on the reader, and the motivations of the characters so much harder to fathom. And so it is with climate science: the caveats, context and cautions scientists attach to their work are forgotten by excited journalists who report it and who furthermore forget their roles as critics of authority, be it political or scientific.

An insidious and self-fulfilling prophecy turns the observation of an unremarkable melting of a few millimetres of ice into a story about several miles of melted ice, and metres of sea-level rise.

The loss of scientific context does something to explain how the significance of scientific research is amplified by stories which cover them. But there is a wider context to scientific research—especially climate research—which a view of the deficit between scientists and journalists does not capture. After all, some scientists are involved to some extent in the creation of dramatic stories about the melting of ice and the peddling of alarm in the media. Following the NASA story, Edward Hannah, reader in climate change at the University of Sheffield, wrote in the *Guardian* that 'the Greenland ice sheet is living on borrowed time', and that 'tens of centimetres' of sea-level rise 'would make many coastal communities more vulnerable to flooding and storm surges'. Such a conclusion had nothing to do with the story at hand and presupposed that it was beyond the means and minds of 'coastal communities' a century hence to move themselves away from the shore or build coastal protection.

It is this historical illiteracy that afflicts scientists as much as it moves journalists to promote alarmist interpretations of press releases from climate science—of which they are equally illiterate. Climate change excites the imaginations of individuals—journalists and scientists included—who labour under a narrative of humanity's close relationship with nature. On this view, 'coastal communities' are incapable of responding to changing circumstances, even over the course of centuries. Thus a theoretical problem that may emerge thousands of years into the future becomes an immediate danger that can only be dealt with now, and in the way preferred by the alarmist narrative: ceasing the industrial and economic progress that would afford those coastal communities a better way of life, as well as better protection from the elements. An insidious and self-fulfilling prophecy turns the observation of an unremarkable melting of a few millimetres of ice into a story about several miles of melted ice, and metres of sea-level rise.

Science cannot tell you that melting ice is significant; it can only explain how much of it has melted.

Damaging Expectations of Science

A belief persists that is possible strictly to set the boundaries of politics and science, such that science can issue politics with imperatives on the basis of what it detects in the material world. But clearly, the poorly conceived environmental narrative and pseudoscientific factoids persist across both science and politics. The damage done by the characterisation of the debate as one between scientists and sceptics, and the view of science and politics as easily delineated processes, is that progress is made in neither politics nor science. Even correcting the excesses of environmental alarmism—or for that matter, climate scepticism—means scientists taking sides in a political war. 'It doesn't matter what you're going to do, you're still going to upset people', says Brandon.

This should give us a clue as to how damaging the expectations of science are. Science is expected to give decisive answers to the debate and unambiguous instructions to politics. Brandon crystallises the problem: 'In a way, it doesn't matter how much you don't want to be part of the public debate', he says. 'You've got no right to be quiet, because the implications of some of the things that people are determining are significant'. The scientist who produces research that either tends towards or against the alarmist picture of the world finds him or herself on that side. So why do any science or make comments in public at all?

As long as there is an expectation that science can only produce uncorrupted and objective accounts of the world, the immediate significance of melting ice (and other things) will continue to be overstated. And while there is an expectation that instructions to politics can be simply read off from scientific observations, anti-progress and anti-human narratives, of the kind epitomised by the Guardian's alarmism, will persist. It is these tendencies which allow a few millimetres of melted ice to turn into stories about several miles of melting, and many meters of sea level rise.

One way out of this impasse might be to recognise the extent to which the dramatic storyline of climate catastrophe precedes science, afflicting even scientists. It's not enough to simply say that this or that aspect of alarmism is overcooked; the problem is with the entire outlook. Science cannot tell you that melting ice is significant; it can only explain how much of it has melted. The significance of melting ice is determined by how much we believe the future depends on ice not melting.

6

Ice Sheets Are Melting at an Increasing Rate

Irene Quaile

Born in Scotland and based in Bonn, Germany, Irene Quaile is an environmental correspondent for German broadcaster Deutsche Welle.

In the last twenty years, the polar ice sheets have melted faster than they have in the last ten thousand years. Data on the Arctic and Antarctic collected from numerous satellites have been combined for the most accurate study on ice loss to date. Melting is fastest in the Arctic ice sheet, where two-thirds of it is occurring in Greenland, which is closer to the equator than Antarctica. It is more complex in Antarctica; on the west, the ice sheet melt is accelerating, but on the east, the ice sheet is growing. Still, this is evidence that climate change is leading to more ocean evaporation and precipitation. Twenty years is a short period to make conclusions on climate change, but scientists see it as a signal of global warming.

The polar regions are important drivers of the world's climate. When the "everlasting ice" melts at an increasing rate, the rest of the world is affected. Global sea levels are rising, dark meltwater pools absorb warmth from the sun which white ice would reflect back into space. Fresh water flows into the sea, changing ocean currents and the living conditions for marine organisms.

For 20 years satellites have been monitoring earth's biggest ice shields on Greenland and in the Antarctic, using different technologies from radar to gravity measurements. In the past, the uncoordinated publication of individual one-off measurements led to confusion, especially with regard to the state of the Antarctic ice. A new study, supported by NASA and European Space Agency ESA combines the data from different satellite missions.

"It's the first time all the people who have estimated changes in the size of the Antarctic and Greenland ice sheets using satellites over the past 20 years have got together to produce a single result," Andrew Shepherd from the University of Leeds in the UK explained in an interview with DW [Deutsche Welle].

Satellite Monitoring Ends Confusion

"Thanks to the accuracy of our data set, we are now able to say with confidence that Antarctica has lost ice for the whole of the past 20 years. In addition to the relative proportions of ice that have been lost in the northern and southern hemispheres, we can also see there's been a definitive acceleration of ice loss in the last 20 years. So together Antarctica and Greenland are now contributing three times as much ice to sea levels as they were 20 years ago," says the Professor of Earth Observation.

According to the study, melting ice from both poles has been responsible for a fifth of the global rise in sea levels since 1992, 11 millimeters in all. The rest was caused by the thermal expansion of the warming ocean, the melting of mountain glaciers, small Arctic ice caps and groundwater mining. The share of the polar ice melt, however, is rising.

Greenland Is Melting Fastest

The pattern of change differs considerably between the Arctic and the Antarctic. Two thirds of the ice loss is happening in Greenland. "The rate of ice loss from Greenland has increased almost five-fold since the mid-1990s", says Erik Ivins, who co-ordinated the project for NASA.

Although the Greenland ice sheet is only about one tenth the size of Antarctica, today it is contributing twice as much ice to sea levels, according to Shepherd: "It's certainly the larger player, probably just because it is at a more equatorial latitude, further from the North pole than Antarctica from the South pole." The ice on Greenland is also melting on the surface, because of increasing air temperatures.

---

20 years is a very short time-scale to draw conclusions about climate change.

Different Conditions Within the Antarctic

In the Antarctic, the situation is a more complex one. Scientists distinguish between the West and East, which are being affected differently by climate change. West Antarctica is losing ice at an accelerating rate. Many of the region's glaciers are by the sea, which is warming. It is only to be expected that the ice is melting faster here, says Shepherd.

In the huge area of East Antartica, the ice is mostly above sea level, Shepherd explains. The air temperature is also much lower, and the experts do not expect the ice to melt on account of rising temperatures. In this part of Antarctica, the ice sheet is actually growing as a consequence of increased snowfall. This has led some critics to question the global warming theory. However for Shepherd and his colleagues, the changes are all consistent with patterns of climate warming, which leads to more evaporation from the oceans and in turn more precipitation, which falls as snow on the ice sheets.

20 Years of Satellites—Too Short to Tell?

20 years is a very short time-scale to draw conclusions about climate change. "We are just beginning an observational record

for ice," said co-author of the study Ian Joughlin, a glaciologist at the University of Washington. "This creates a new long-term data set that will increase as new measurements are made."

But the scientists are convinced the relatively new technology is the best way to keep track of climate change in inaccessible polar regions. Earth observation expert Shepherd is sure global warming is the only possible explanation for the accelerating polar ice melt. He sees especially the rapid melt in West Antarctica as a signal and a result of direct changes in the local balance between the ice sheet, the ocean and the atmosphere.

If the west Antarctic ice sheet should become unstable, it could trigger abrupt changes globally. Joughlin sees the recent ice activity in the region as a reason to pay attention, but not to panic.

Key Data for the IPCC

In the last report by the IPCC (Intergovernmental Panel on Climate Change), the development of the ice sheets was regarded as the major unknown factor with regard to predicting future sea level rises. "The results of this study will be invaluable in informing the IPCC as it completes the writing of its Fifth Assessment Report next year," according to Tom Wagner, NASA's cryosphere program manager in Washington.

The question of how the satellite data will influence predictions of sea level rise is not easy to answer, says Andrew Shepherd: Any model is only as reliable as its data. He hopes the more accurate satellite measurements will help improve the models. He does, however, have one reservation. The main uncertainty in climate projections is not to do with the physics or processes, the scientist says. It is the uncertainty as to what emissions scenarios nations will adopt in the future.

7

The Melting of Glaciers Cannot Be Reversed with Global Warming

Bharat Raj Singh and Onkar Singh

Bharat Raj Singh is a professor and director of School of Management Sciences, Technical Campus, Lucknow, Uttar Pradesh, India. Onkar Singh is a professor at Harcourt Butler Technological Institute, Kanpur, Uttar Pradesh, India.

Ice sheets and glaciers are more vulnerable to climate change than previously estimated. According to a recent study, the Greenland ice sheet may completely melt if a temperature threshold of 1.6 degrees Celsius above preindustrial levels is reached—a rise of 0.8 degrees Celsius has already been recorded. Satellite images also reveal that Arctic sea ice has retreated to a record low in August 2012, and scientists predict that it will disappear during the summers in two decades. Research reveals that 70 percent of sea ice loss in the Arctic results from man-made climate change. These findings are an alarm call for significant reductions in carbon emissions and a focus on renewable energy sources.

Earth's climate changes naturally and such changes in the intensity of sunlight reaching the earth cause cycles of warming and cooling that have been a regular feature of the Earth's climatic history. Some of these solar cycles—like the four glacial-interglacial swings during the past 400,000 years—

Bharat Raj Singh and Onkar Singh, "Chapter 2: A Study About Realities of Climate Change: Glacier Melting and Growing Crises," *Climate Change—Realities, Impacts Over Ice Cap, Sea Level and Risks,* inTech Publisher, 51000 Rijeka, Croatia, 2013, pp. 42, 45–50. Copyright © 2013 by Bharat Raj Singh and Onkar Singh. All rights reserved. Reproduced by permission.

extend over very long time scales and can have large amplitudes of 5 to 6°C. For the past 10,000 years, the earth has been in the warm interglacial phase of such a cycle. Other solar cycles are much shorter, with the shortest being the 11 year sunspot cycle. Other natural causes of climate change include variations in ocean currents (which can alter the distribution of heat and precipitation) and large eruptions of volcanoes (which can sporadically increase the concentration of atmospheric particles, blocking out more sunlight). Still, for thousands of years, the Earth's atmosphere has changed very little. Temperature and the balance of heat-trapping greenhouse gases have remained just right for humans, animals and plants to survive. But today we're having problems keeping this balance, because we burn fossil fuels to heat our homes, run our cars, produce electricity, and manufacture all sorts of products, we're adding more greenhouse gases to the atmosphere. By increasing the amount of these gases, the warming capability of the natural greenhouse effect is enhanced. It's the human-induced enhanced greenhouse effect that causes environmental concern, because it has the potential to warm the planet at a rate that has never been experienced in human history. . . .

Greenland Ice Sheet May Melt Completely with 1.6 Degrees of Global Warming

The Greenland ice sheet is likely to be more vulnerable to global warming than previously thought. The temperature threshold for melting the ice sheet completely is in the range of 0.8 to 3.2 degrees Celsius of global warming, with a best estimate of 1.6 degrees above pre-industrial levels, shows a new study by scientists from the Potsdam Institute for Climate Impact Research (PIK) and the Universidad Complutense de Madrid. Today, already 0.8 degrees of global warming has been observed. Substantial melting of land ice could contribute to long-term sea-level rise of several meters and therefore it potentially affects the lives of many millions of people.

The time it takes before most of the ice in Greenland is lost strongly depends on the level of warming. "The more we exceed the threshold, the faster it melts," says Alexander Robinson, lead-author of the study now published in *Nature Climate Change*. In a business-as-usual scenario of greenhouse-gas emissions, in the long run humanity might be aiming at 8 degrees Celsius of global warming. This would result in one fifth of the ice sheet melting within 500 years and a complete loss in 2000 years, according to the study. "This is not what one would call a rapid collapse," says Robinson. "However, compared to what has happened in our planet's history, it is fast. And we might already be approaching the critical threshold."

If the global temperature significantly overshoots the threshold for a long time, the ice [in Greenland] will continue melting and not regrow—even if the climate would, after many thousand years, return to its pre-industrial state.

In contrast, if global warming would be limited to 2 degrees Celsius, complete melting would happen on a timescale of 50,000 years. Still, even within this temperature range often considered a global guardrail, the Greenland ice sheet is not secure. Previous research suggested a threshold in global temperature increase for melting the Greenland ice sheet of a best estimate of 3.1 degrees, with a range of 1.9 to 5.1 degrees. The new study's best estimate indicates about half as much.

"Our study shows that under certain conditions the melting of the Greenland ice sheet becomes irreversible. This supports the notion that the ice sheet is a tipping element in the Earth system," says team-leader Andrey Ganopolski of PIK. "If the global temperature significantly overshoots the threshold for a long time, the ice will continue melting and not regrow—even if the climate would, after many thousand years, return to its preindustrial state." This is related to feedbacks between the climate and the ice sheet: The ice sheet is over 3000 meters thick and thus elevated into cooler altitudes. . . . When it melts its surface comes down to lower altitudes with higher temperatures, which accelerates the melting. Also, the ice reflects a large part of solar radiation back into space. When the area covered by ice decreases, more radiation is absorbed and this adds to regional warming.

The scientists achieved insights by using a novel computer simulation of the Greenland ice sheet and the regional climate. This model performs calculations of these physical systems including the most important processes, for instance climate feedbacks associated with changes in snowfall and melt under global warming. The simulation proved able to correctly calculate both the observed ice-sheet of today and its evolution over previous glacial cycles, thus increasing the confidence that it can properly assess the future. All this makes the new estimate of Greenland temperature threshold more reliable than previous ones. . . .

Arctic Sea Ice Shrinks to Smallest Extent Ever Recorded

Sea ice in the Arctic has shrunk to its smallest extent ever recorded, smashing the previous record minimum and prompting warnings of accelerated climate change. Satellite images show that the rapid summer melt has reduced the area of frozen sea to less than 3.5 million square kilometres this week from 27 August 2012—less than half the area typically occupied four decades ago. Arctic sea ice cover has been shrinking since the 1970s when it averaged around 8m sq km a year, but such a dramatic collapse in ice cover in one year is highly unusual.

A record low in 2007 of 4.17 million sq km was broken on Monday, 27 August 2012; further melting has since amounted to more than 500,000 sq km. The record, which is based on a five-day average, is expected to be officially declared in the next few days by the National Snow and Ice Data Centre (NSIDC) in Colorado. The NSIDC's data shows the sea ice extent is bumping along the bottom, with a new low of 3.421m sq km on Tuesday, which rose very slightly to 3.429m sq km on Wednesday and 3.45m sq km on Thursday. . . .

Scientists have predicted on 31st August 2012 that the Arctic Ocean could be ice-free in summer months within 20 years, leading to possibly major climate impacts. "I am surprised. This is an indication that the Arctic sea ice cover is fundamentally changing. The trends all show less ice and thinner ice," said Julienne Stroeve, a research scientist with the NSIDC.

The disappearance of Arctic ice is the most visible warning sign of the need to tackle climate change and ensure we have a world fit to pass on to the next generation.

"We are on the edge of one of the most significant moments in environmental history as sea ice heads towards a new record low. The loss of sea ice will be devastating, raising global temperatures that will impact on our ability to grow food and causing extreme weather around the world," said John Sauven, director of Greenpeace UK.

Sea ice experts said that they were surprised by the collapse because weather conditions were not conducive to a major melt this year. The ice is now believed to be much thinner than it used to be and easier to melt.

Arctic sea ice follows an annual cycle of melting through the warm summer months and refreezing in the winter. The sea ice plays a critical role in regulating climate, acting as a giant mirror that reflects much of the Sun's energy, helping to cool the Earth.

David Nussbaum, chief executive of WWF-UK, said: "The disappearance of Arctic ice is the most visible warning sign of the need to tackle climate change and ensure we have a world fit to pass on to the next generation. The sheer scale of ice loss is shocking and unprecedented. This alarm call from the Arctic needs to reverberate across Whitehall and boardrooms. We can all take action to cut carbon emissions and move towards a 100% renewable economy."

Ed Davey, the UK climate and energy secretary, said: "These findings highlight the urgency for the international community to act. We understand that Arctic sea-ice decline has accelerated over recent years as global warming continues to increase Arctic temperatures at a faster rate than the global average.

"This Government is working hard to tackle climate change and we are working closely with our international partners not to exceed 2 degrees above pre industrial levels. I am calling for the EU to increase its emission target from 20% to 30% and will be taking an active lead at the UNFCCC [United Nations Framework Convention on Climate Change] Climate change talks in Doha later this year, where I will push for further progress towards a new global deal on climate change and for more mitigation action now. The fact is that we cannot afford to wait."

Canadian scientists said that the record melt this year could lead to a cold winter in the UK and Europe, as the heat in the Arctic water will be released into the atmosphere this autumn, potentially affecting the all-important jet stream. While the science is still developing in this area, the Met Office said in May that the reduction in Arctic sea ice was contributing in part to the colder, drier winters the UK has been experiencing in recent years. . . .

Loss of Arctic Sea Ice Mostly Due to Human Causes

[The] study finds only 30% of radical loss of summer sea ice is due to natural variability in Atlantic—and it will probably get worse. Since the 1970s, there has been a 40% decrease in the extent of summer sea ice. The radical decline in sea ice around the Arctic is at least 70% due to human-induced climate change, according to a new study, and may even be up to 95% [due] to humans—rather higher than scientists had previously thought. The loss of ice around the Arctic has adverse effects on wildlife and also opens up new northern sea routes and opportunities to drill for oil and gas under the newly accessible sea bed. . . . The reduction has been accelerating since the 1990s and many scientists believe the Arctic may become ice-free in the summers later this century, possibly as early as the late 2020s.

"Since the 1970s, there's been a 40% decrease in the summer sea ice extent," said Jonny Day, a climate scientist at the National Centre for Atmospheric Science at the University of Reading, who led the latest study.

"We were trying to determine how much of this was due to natural variability and therefore imply what aspect is due to man-made climate change as well."

To test the ideas, Day carried out several computer-based simulations of how the climate around the Arctic might have fluctuated since 1979 without the input of greenhouse gases from human activity.

He found that a climate system called the Atlantic multidecadal oscillation (AMO) was a dominant source of variability in ice extent. The AMO is a cycle of warming and cooling in the North Atlantic that repeats every 65 to 80 years—it has been in a warming phase since the mid-1970s.

Comparing the models with actual observations, Day was able to work out what contribution the natural systems had made to what researchers have observed from satellite data.

"We could only attribute as much as 30% [of the Arctic ice loss] to the AMO," he said. "Which implies that the rest is due to something else, and this is most likely going to be man-made global change?"

Previous studies had indicated that around half of the loss was due to man-made climate change and that the other half was due to natural variability. Looking across all his simulations, Day found that the 30% figure was an upper limit—the AMO could have contributed as little as 5% to the overall loss of Arctic ice in recent decades.

The research is published online in the journal *Environmental Research Letters*. Day said that there are a number of feedback effects that could see the Arctic ice loss continue in the coming years, as the Earth warms up. "[There is] something called the ice-albedo feedback, which means that when you have less ice, it means there's more open water and therefore the ocean absorbs more radiation and will continue to warm," he said.

"It's unclear what will happen—it definitely seems like it's going in that direction."

8

Ice Sheets Are Not Collapsing

Cliff Ollier

Cliff Ollier is a geologist, geomorphologist, and professor emeritus at the University of Western Australia.

Contrary to alarmist warnings of climate change, the ice sheets in the Arctic and Antarctic are not at risk of collapsing. Such claims are founded on concepts that are false. According to the most common notion, glaciers slide downhill—lubricated by meltwater—leading to widespread melting and rising sea levels. The ice sheets in Greenland and the Antarctic, however, are located in deep basins and must flow uphill. Moreover, the rate of ice flow represents the amount of ice accumulated and is not dependent on present climate conditions. In addition, ice sheets melt at the edges not on the surface, and such melting reflects past rates of snow and ice accumulation in their interior and is not an indication they are collapsing. All these factors suggest that the world's ice sheets are not in a state of collapse.

In these days of warnings about climate change, the ice sheets of Greenland and Antarctica play an important role. [Researcher] Alan Carlin wrote, [director of NASA's Goddard Institute for Space Studies James] "Hansen et al. believe that the most likely and most critical of these dangerous effects is the possibility of substantial sea level rise due to the breakup of parts or all of the ice sheets covering Greenland and West Antarctica."

Cliff Ollier, "Glaciers—Science and Nonsense," *Geoscientist*, Vol. 20, No. 3, March 2010. Copyright © 2010 by Geological Society of London. All rights reserved. Reproduced by permission.

Alarm started with "global warming" but since the Earth failed to warm in the past 10 years, it changed to "climate change" and most recently to "carbon pollution." But the most graphic scare is still of rising sea levels, so many articles continue to appear describing sea level rise of many metres caused by the melting of the icesheets.

Like the original warming scares, the melting scares are based on models, and poor models at that. The commonest one is the notion that glaciers slide downhill, lubricated by meltwater, and that this can pass a threshold and lead to melting of all the icesheets and a runaway rise in sea level. The sliding hypothesis was the best available to [Swiss physicist Horace-Bénédict] De Saussure, but we have learned a lot since then—but it has been forgotten again in many modern models.

It may take many thousands of years for ice to flow from the accumulation area to the melting area. The balance between movement and melting, therefore, does not relate to today's climate, but to the climate thousands of years ago.

The mechanism of glacier flow was long controversial, as observers tried to reconcile the solidness of ice with its ability to flow as a non-rigid body. Early experimenters placed lines of sticks across glaciers and found the middle moved faster than the edges—there was plasticity in the ice. Fierce controversies raged and brought in occasional new aspects of physics (such as regelation), but it was not until the crystallography of ice could be studied that real progress was made. The crystals in a glacier take on a preferred orientation as they travel down glacier. The crystals of ice at the glacier terminus may be a thousand times bigger than those at the source. How can this be? Scientist in the 1940s such as Max Perutz (a Nobel Prize winner in Physics, not Peace!) explained glaciers as being like a metamorphic rock consisting of one mineral, which flowed by a process called creep (and incidentally developed petrofabric properties not explained in other models).

It is also worth noting the geometry and age of the great icecaps. The Greenland, East Antarctica and West Antarctica ice sheets occupy kilometre-deep basins, and the ice cannot possibly slide downhill—it has to flow uphill. In simple numbers, the Greenland icecap has existed for three million years and the Antarctic Ice sheets 30 million. Why such contrast between the two hemispheres? The idea that both simply respond to average temperatures of today is oversimplified.

Glacier Budget

Glaciers grow, flow and melt continuously, with a budget of gains and losses. Snow falls on high ground. It compacts with time, air is extruded, and it turns into solid ice. More precipitation of snow forms another layer on the top, which goes through the same process, so the ice grows thicker by the addition of new layers at the surface. This stratified ice preserves data on temperature and carbon dioxide over hundreds of thousands of years. When the ice is thick enough it starts to flow under the force of gravity, and when it reaches a lower altitude or latitude where temperature is higher, it starts to melt and evaporate (ablate).

If growth and melting balance, the glacier appears to be "stationary." If precipitation exceeds melting, the glacier advances: if melting exceeds precipitation the glacier recedes, but there will be a time lag between cause and effect.

In ice sheets, it may take many thousands of years for ice to flow from the accumulation area to the melting area. The balance between movement and melting, therefore, does not relate to today's climate, but to the climate thousands of years ago.

How Glaciers Move

Glacier flow is by a process called creep, essentially the movement of molecules from one crystal to another. Ice crystals are in the hexagonal system with glide planes parallel to the base. In lake ice, the c-axes are vertical and the glide planes all parallel to the lake surface, so a push parallel to the glide planes deforms the ice readily. Greater stress is needed to deform ice perpendicularly to these glide planes. In the absence of any stress, an individual grain of ice will lose as many molecules as it gains, and so remain unchanged. A stressed crystal will lose more molecules than it gains and so shrink, while a nearby unstressed grain will gain more than it loses, and grow. In this way, glacier ice acquires a preferred petrofabric orientation. The ice crystals at a glacier snout have a volume about a thousand times greater than that of the first-formed ice crystals at the source of the glacier. These observations cannot be explained by mechanisms that ignore the creep mechanism of glacier flow. . . .

There Is No Surface Melting of Icecaps

The stratified ice is of great age. In Greenland, several ice-cores have more than 3km [1.9 miles] of undisturbed ice which go back in time for over 105,000 years—far less than the Antarctic equivalent. The Vostok cores in Antarctica provide data for the past 414,000 years before the ice starts to deform by flow. Dome F core reached 3035 m [9957 feet] and Dome C core 3309 m [10,856 feet], both dating back to 720,000 years. The EPICA core in Antarctica goes back to 760,000 years, and retains complete records of deposition, although temperatures at times during that period have been higher than today. They do not fit a model of surface melting, either now or in the past. After three-quarters of a million years of documented continuous accumulation, how can we believe that right now the world's ice sheets are "collapsing"?

Glacial Surges

Climate alarmists note some glaciers that have increased in speed, and attribute it directly to climate warming. It is much better explained, however, by known laws of creep. The speed of valley glaciers is rather variable. Sometimes a valley glacier will flow several times faster than it did earlier. Suppose we had a long period of heavy precipitation. This would cause a thickening of the ice, and more rapid glacial flow. The pulse of more rapid flow would eventually pass down the valley. The increase in flow rate is not related to present day air temperature, but to increased precipitation long ago. Hubbard Glacier surged in 1986, at the height of the global warming that took place between 1975 and 1998.

Pulling Glaciers to the Sea

A number of papers give the impression that melting of glacial ice at the sea somehow causes the glacier to flow faster. Hubbard Glacier is the largest tidewater glacier on the North American continent. Since it was first mapped in 1895 it has been thickening and advancing (at a rate of 25m [82 feet] per year), even though smaller glaciers in the vicinity have been retreating. Why?

The point to remember is that the release of icebergs at the edge of an ice cap does not in any way reflect present-day temperature.

One "explanation" [from the US Geological Survey] says: "This atypical behaviour is an important example of a calving glacier cycle in which glacier advance and retreat is controlled more by the mechanics of terminus calving than by climate fluctuations." But glaciers are pushed by the weight of the glacier, not sucked by the calving at the ice front, and destruction at the ice front does not depend on present day climate. And why should calving cause an advance?

The cause of the advance is most likely that the glacier has been thickening since 1895, a feature described since the first observations were made.

The Breakup of Ice Sheets

Wherever ice sheets or glaciers reach the sea, the ice floats and eventually breaks off to form icebergs. It is part of the glacial budget: the glaciers never flowed on to the equator. Icebergs have always been with us, and Captain [James] Cook saw icebergs on his search for the great south land.

Yet we are shown many movies of ice sheets collapsing, and are told it is a sign of global warming. In fact although the break-up of ice sheets is simply part of the glacier budget, observers seem surprised by the size and suddenness of what they see. In 2007, when a piece of the Greenland ice shelf broke away, interviewed scientists said they were surprised at how suddenly it happened. How else but suddenly would a piece of ice shelf break off? The actual break is inevitably a sudden event—but one that can easily be built into a global warming horror scenario. The point to remember is that the release of icebergs at the edge of an ice cap does not in any way reflect present-day temperature.

The Hubbard Glacier in Alaska has long been a favourite place for tourists to witness the collapse of an ice front 10km [6.2 miles] long and 27m [88.5 feet] high, sometimes producing icebergs the size of ten-storey buildings. One tourist wrote, "Hubbard Glacier is very active and we didn't have long to wait for it to calve." Yet the Hubbard Glacier is advancing at 25 m [82 feet] per year!

It is easy to raise alarms over a large break. In 2009 Peter Garrett [Australian Minister for the Environment] claimed the break-up of the Wilkins ice shelf in West Antarctica "indicated sea level rises of 6 m were possible by the end of the century, and that ice was melting across the continent". Actually, when floating ice melts there is no change in sea level (by Archimedes' Principle).

Ice Sheet "Collapse"

Claims that ice sheets "collapse" are based on false concepts. Glaciers do not slide on their bellies, lubricated by meltwater. Ice sheets do not melt from the surface down—they melt only at the edges. Once the edges are lost, further loss depends on the rate of flow of the ice. The rate of flow of ice does not depend on the present climate, but on the amount of ice already accumulated, and the ice sheet will keep flowing for a very long time. The ice cores show that the stratified ice has accumulated over half a million years and has not been deformed, remelted or "collapsed." Variations in melting around the edges of ice sheets are no indication that they are collapsing, but reflect past rates of snow and ice accumulation in their interior. Indeed "collapse" is impossible.

9

Antarctica Is Melting

Erik Conway

Erik Conway is the historian at NASA's Jet Propulsion Laboratory at the California Institute of Technology in Pasadena.

The latest satellite data reveals that West Antarctica is losing mass despite a decrease in surface melting. Nonetheless, ice flow can occur without such melting. In glaciology, it is theorized that ice shelves hold back glaciers, slowing their movements to the ocean. The disintegration of ice shelves—caused by the melting of their undersides and ice flowing downhill—allows the flow of glaciers to accelerate. Additionally, thinner shelves are more vulnerable to crumbling. Furthermore, warming waters around Antarctica may also contribute to the breaking of ice shelves. The continent is in fact losing mass at an increasing rate, according to the data.

There has been lots of talk lately about Antarctica and whether or not the continent's giant ice sheet is melting. One new paper, which states there's less surface melting recently than in past years, has been cited as "proof" that there's no global warming. Other evidence that the amount of sea ice around Antarctica seems to be increasing slightly is being used in the same way. But both of these data points are misleading. Gravity data collected from space using NASA's Grace satellite show that Antarctica has been losing more than a hundred cubic kilometers (24 cubic miles) of ice each year since 2002. The latest data reveal that Antarctica is losing ice at an accel-

Erik Conway, "Is Antarctica Melting?," www.nasa.gov, January 12, 2010.

erating rate, too. How is it possible for surface melting to decrease, but for the continent to lose mass anyway? The answer boils down to the fact that ice can flow without melting.

Two-thirds of Antarctica is a high, cold desert. Known as East Antarctica, this section has an average altitude of about 2 kilometer (1.2 miles), higher than the American Colorado Plateau. There is a continent about the size of Australia underneath all this ice; the ice sheet sitting on top averages at a little over 2 kilometer (1.2 miles) thick. If all of this ice melted, it would raise global sea level by about 60 meters (197 feet). But little, if any, surface warming is occurring over East Antarctica. Radar and laser-based satellite data show a little mass loss at the edges of East Antarctica, which is being partly offset by accumulation of snow in the interior, although a very recent result from the NASA/German Aerospace Center's Gravity Recovery and Climate Experiment (Grace) suggests that since 2006 there has been more ice loss from East Antarctica than previously thought. Overall, not much is going on in East Antarctica—yet.

[The] dynamic process of ice flowing downhill to the sea is what enables Antarctica to continue losing mass even as surface melting declines.

A Frozen Hawaii

West Antarctica is very different. Instead of a single continent, it is a series of islands covered by ice—think of it as a frozen Hawaii, with penguins. Because it's a group of islands, much of the West Antarctic Ice Sheet (WAIS, in the jargon) is actually sitting on the floor of the Southern Ocean, not on dry land. Parts of it are more than 1.7 kilometer (1 mile) below sea level. Pine Island is the largest of these islands and the largest ice stream in West Antarctica is called Pine Island Glacier. The WAIS, if it melted completely, would raise sea level by 5 to 7 meter (16 to 23 feet). And the Pine Island Glacier would contribute about 10 percent of that.

Since the early 1990s, European and Canadian satellites have been collecting radar data from West Antarctica. These radar data can reveal ice motion and, by the late 1990s, there was enough data for scientists to measure the annual motion of the Pine Island Glacier. Using radar information collected between 1992 and 1996, oceanographer Eric Rignot, based at NASA's Jet Propulsion Laboratory (JPL), found that the Pine Island Glacier's "grounding line"—the line between the glacier's floating section and the part of the glacier that rests on the sea floor—had retreated rapidly towards the land. That meant that the glacier was losing mass. He attributed the retreat to the warming waters around West Antarctica. But with only a few years of data, he couldn't say whether the retreat was a temporary, natural anomaly or a longer-term trend from global warming.

Rignot's paper surprised many people. JPL scientist Ron Kwok saw it as demonstrating that "the old idea that glaciers move really slowly isn't true any more." One result was that a lot more people started to use the radar data to examine much more of Antarctica. A major review published in 2009 found that Rignot's Pine Island Glacier finding hadn't been a fluke: a large majority of the marine glaciers of the Antarctic Peninsula were retreating, and their retreat was speeding up. This summer [in 2010], a British group revisited the Pine Island Glacier finding and found that its rate of retreat had quadrupled between 1995 and 2006.

How the Ice Shelf Crumbles

The retreat of West Antarctica's glaciers is being accelerated by ice shelf collapse. Ice shelves are the part of a glacier that extends past the grounding line towards the ocean; they are the most vulnerable to warming seas. A longstanding theory in glaciology is that these ice shelves tend to buttress (support the end wall of) glaciers, with their mass slowing the ice movement towards the sea, and this was confirmed by the spectacular collapse of the Rhode Island-sized Larsen B shelf along the Eastern edge of the Antarctic Peninsula in 2002. The disintegration, which was caught on camera by NASA's Moderate Resolution Imaging Spectroradiometer (MODIS) imaging instruments on board its Terra and Aqua satellites, was dramatic: it took just three weeks to crumble a 12,000-year old ice shelf. Over the next few years, satellite radar data showed that some of the ice streams flowing behind Larsen B had accelerated significantly, while others, still supported by smaller ice shelves, had not. This dynamic process of ice flowing downhill to the sea is what enables Antarctica to continue losing mass even as surface melting declines.

Michael Schodlok, a JPL scientist who models the way ice shelves and the ocean interact, says melting of the underside of the shelf is a pre-requisite to these collapses. Thinning of the ice shelf reduces its buttressing effect on the glacier behind it, allowing glacier flow to speed up. The thinner shelf is also more likely to crack. In the summer, meltwater ponds on the surface can drain into the cracks. Since liquid water is denser than solid ice, enough meltwater on the surface can open the cracks up deeper down into the ice, leading to disintegration of the shelf. The oceans surrounding Antarctica have been warming, so Schodlok doesn't doubt that the ice shelves are being undermined by warmer water being brought up from the depths. But he admits that it hasn't been proven rigorously, because satellites can't measure underneath the ice.

Glaciologist Robert Bindschadler of NASA's Goddard Space Flight Center intends to show just that. He's leading an expedition scheduled to start in 2011 to drill through the Pine Island Glacier and place an automated buoy into the water below it. According to Bindschadler, Pine Island Glacier "is the place to go because that is where the changes are the largest. If we want to understand how the ocean is impacting the ice sheet, go to where it's hitting the ice sheet with a sledgeham-mer, not with a little tack hammer."

Meanwhile, measurements from the Grace satellites con-firm that Antarctica is losing mass. Isabella Velicogna of JPL and the University of California, Irvine, uses Grace data to weigh the Antarctic ice sheet from space. Her work shows that the ice sheet is not only losing mass, but it is losing mass at an accelerating rate. "The important message is that it is not a linear trend. A linear trend means you have the same mass loss every year. The fact that it's above linear, this is the im-portant idea, that ice loss is increasing with time," she says. And she points out that it isn't just the Grace data that show accelerating loss; the radar data do, too. "It isn't just one type of measurement. It's a series of independent measurements that are giving the same results, which makes it more robust."

10

Antarctica Is Not Melting

Marc Sheppard

Marc Sheppard is former environmental editor of American Thinker.

Climate change alarmists warn that Antarctic ice shelves are melting due to warming ocean temperatures, which will lead to a catastrophic rise in sea levels. But their claims are plagued by several problems. First, the evidence—the collapse of ice shelves— focuses on the Antarctic Peninsula, located in the volcanically active South Atlantic. In addition, researchers that sought to determine if northeastern ice shelves are also melting at the same rate—as claimed by alarmists—found that the water beneath is near freezing point and has not warmed. As a matter of fact, in Antarctica, air temperatures have remained below zero and water temperatures have remained near freezing, contradicting assertions that global warming will impact polar regions the most.

On Monday [January 10, 2010], scientists from the Norwegian Polar Institute [NPI] reported that they'd measured sea temperatures beneath an East Antarctic ice shelf and found no signs of warming whatsoever. And while the discovery's corollaries remain mostly blurred by the few rogue mainstream media outlets actually reporting it, the findings are in fact yet another serious blow to the sky-is-falling-because-oceans-are-rising prophecies of the climate alarm crowd.

For years now, alarmists have insisted that Antarctica is thawing thanks to man-made global warming. They warn that such melting of a frozen continent containing 90 percent of all the ice on the planet would inevitably lead to a cataclysmic sea level rise (SLR). Scary stuff, indeed.

However, there are several problems with their assertions, not the least of which is that all evidence of melting selectively focuses on the only area of the continent satellite evidence confirms is warming—the western region in general, and the Antarctic Peninsula in particular.

But as ICECAP's [International Climate and Environmental Change Assessment Project] Joe D'Aleo observed in 2008, the relatively small area of the peninsula offers an extremely poor representative sample, as it juts out well north of the mainland into an area of the South Atlantic well known for its "surface and subsurface active volcanic activity." And in the greater scheme, adds D'Aleo, "the vast continent has actually cooled since 1979."

Still, carbo-chondriacs blame the "collapse" of ten ice shelves in and around the peninsula on melting of the underside of the ice by global-warming-fueled rising ocean temperatures. And they insist that their models are spot-on in predicting that unless mankind stops pumping CO_2 into the atmosphere, it's only a matter of time before the entire continent melts. The effect of such an event, they caution, would be nothing short of a civilization-ending, 57-meter SLR—a vision normally reserved to biblical fables or the wild imagination of [former vice president and environmental activist] Al Gore.

Northeastern Ice Shelves Not on the Decline

Of course, narrowly isolated melting doesn't support the hypothesis of widespread polar warming necessary to kindle such horrific images of metropolises submerged by anthropogenic impropriety. That's why locating and denouncing diminishing ice east of the Transantarctic Mountains ranks high on every green-funded researcher's to-do list. And that's also why it would appear that NPI scientists thought they had hit the jackpot when their models calculated that the ice shelves at Dronning Maud Land along Antarctica's northeastern border should be melting at the same rate as those farther west.

So last November, a team from NPI set out to investigate the status of just such a locale—the Fimbul Ice Shelf. Their stated primary mission: to determine whether ice masses on the shelf are indeed currently on the decline.

Last month, the expedition drilled its first borehole into the 250-to-400-meter-thick floating ice in order to study the melting and ocean circulation underneath. But readings revealed by the instruments they lowered into the water below were not quite what was anticipated.

> *In contrast to model forecasts, Antarctic ice shelf collapse still appears to be isolated to a very tiny area in the western region of a continent otherwise experiencing continued glacial and ice shelf advancement.*

In fact, contrary to the warmer, ice-melting temperatures predicted by models, NPI oceanographer and project leader Ole Anders Nøst reported that "the water under the ice shelf is very close to the freezing point." Furthermore, there seemed to have been no change in almost five years:

> We observed a roughly 50 meter deep layer of water with temperatures very close to the freezing point, about −2.05 degrees, just beneath the ice shelf. The highest observed temperature was about −1.83 degrees close to the bottom. The temperatures are very similar to temperature data collected by [equipment attached to] elephant seals in 2008 and by British Antarctic Survey using an autosub below the ice shelf in 2005.

Nøst concluded that "This situation seems to be stable, suggesting that the melting under the ice shelf does not increase."

As to the ocean circulation models that incorrectly showed "warm deep water flowing in under the ice shelves," Nøst admitted that "as this is not observed, the models are most likely wrong and should be improved."

Translation: In contrast to model forecasts, Antarctic ice shelf collapse still appears to be isolated to a very tiny area in the western region of a continent otherwise experiencing continued glacial and ice shelf advancement.

Other than select ice shelves . . . in one minuscule area soaking in water warmed by volcanic activity, Antarctica isn't melting at all.

Casting Further Doubt on Sea Level Predictions

And that fact certainly casts further serious doubt on the U.N.'s most recent century-end SLR predictions. Last year, the 18- to 59-centimeter estimate that appeared in the Intergovernmental Panel on Climate Change (IPCC) 2007 Fourth Assessment Report (AR4) was increased to a full two meters, *based entirely on fears of accelerated glacial melting in Greenland and Antarctica.* Keep in mind that since the prolonged cold snap of the Little Ice Age ended in 1850, the global rate of SLR has remained essentially steady at approximately seven inches per century, due largely to thermal expansion.

Reality check time: Does anything in this [analysis] suggest to you that SLR might increase over *tenfold*—as the IPCC now predicts—this century?

As such, is it any wonder that alarmists now claim that even a few degrees of warming will ignite enough accelerated liquefying of the petatons of Earth's surface ice to render the planet barely inhabitable by land-dwellers?

In fact, it was just months after the release of AR4 that the Union of Concerned Scientists [UCS] offered these hyperactive projections to the 2007 U.N. Framework Convention on Climate Change in Bali:

> Sustained warming of [2°C above pre-industrial levels] could, for example, result in the extinction of many species and extensive melting of the Greenland and West Antarctic ice sheets—causing global sea level to rise between 12 and 40 feet.

Readers should be aware that the WAIS sheets UCS referred to are not to be confused with aforementioned ice shelves. While melting "sheets," which predominately lie above bedrock, might contribute to SLR, the ice "shelves" float atop the water and therefore have ostensibly the same impact on SLR frozen as they would melted. There has, however, been concern expressed that melting glaciers might flow faster toward the ocean if unencumbered by the barricading effect of the shelves.

Now, even the notoriously alarmist U.K. Met Office admits that the complete Greenland meltdown to which they'd attribute a seven-meter SLR "would take thousands of years" even if temperatures were to continue to climb. It's therefore quite logical to assume that the majority of the predicted SLR is expected to originate in Antarctica.

And yet, other than select ice shelves (which again are already afloat and would have no further impact upon SLR) in one minuscule area soaking in water warmed by volcanic activity, Antarctica isn't melting at all. And with air temperatures averaging consistently below zero and water temperatures barely above freezing—even in summer—nothing in the foreseeable future suggests it might . . . not even should temperatures, which have been falling since 1998, nonetheless rise to the mostly arbitrary yet internationally alarmist-approved catastrophic level of 2°C above pre-industrial levels.

The Next Soggy
Doom-and-Gloom Prophecy

In fact, despite the IPCC insistence that global warming will be most prevalent at the poles, southern-hemisphere sea ice area has remained virtually unchanged since satellite sensors and analytical programs were first capable of measuring it in 1979.

So perhaps when the green-gospel-pronouncing IPCC releases its Fifth Assessment Report, tentatively due for 2014, contributors and lead authors alike might carefully consider the NPI findings, the steady rate of SLR over the past 150 years, and the overall resilience of Antarctic ice before formulating their next soggy doom-and-gloom prophecy. (And don't forget this undeniable fact: Across the continent, the 2008–2009 southern hemisphere summer hosted the lowest Antarctic ice melt in thirty years.)

Surely were these people bound by scientific concerns exclusively, there'd be no doubt whatsoever that they'd do just that.

11

Global Warming: Impact of Receding Snow and Ice Surprises Scientists

Pete Spotts

Pete Spotts is a science reporter for the Christian Science Monitor.

According to a 2011 study, the Northern Hemisphere's cryosphere, regions that are frozen sometime during the year, is declining in ice and snow cover at more than twice the estimated rate. This study also confirms that feedbacks are stronger, in which ice and snow are reduced through the exposure of heat-absorbing water and land to sunlight during non-winter seasons. This decline decreases the amount of solar energy reflected by the cryosphere back into space, or albedo, speeding up global warming's effects. The melting is expanding, and a significant decrease in the cryosphere's cooling effect, linked to a 1 degree Celsius increase in Northern Hemisphere temperatures, has taken researchers by surprise.

A long-term retreat in snow and ice cover in the Northern Hemisphere is weakening the ability of these seasonal cloaks of white to reflect sunlight back into space and cool global climate, according to a study published this week.

Indeed, over the past 30 years, the cooling effect from this so-called cryosphere—essentially areas covered by snow and ice at least part of the year—appears to have weakened at more than twice the pace projected by global climate models, the research team conducting the work estimates.

The study, which appeared online Sunday in the journal *Nature Geoscience*, represents a first cut at trying to calculate from direct measurements the impact of climate change on the Northern Hemisphere's cryosphere. The study was conducted by a team of federal and university scientists who examined data gathered between 1979 and 2008.

Of particular interest is a self-reinforcing process, or feedback, through which warming reduces snow and ice cover. Those reductions expose more ocean and landscape to sunlight during spring, summer and fall. After absorbing the sunlight, these exposed features radiate the heat back into the atmosphere. This accelerates the loss of snow and ice already triggered by global warming.

Because the Arctic is warmer than its southern counterpart, small changes in temperatures at the top of the world have a relatively larger effect on ice and snow cover.

Pinning down the size of this effect—one of three major feedbacks in the global climate process—is important in understanding how much the global climate could warm in response to rising concentrations of greenhouse gases that human activities have pumped into the atmosphere, explains Mark Serreze, director of the National Snow and Ice Data Center in Boulder, Colo.

Over the past decade or more, other teams have tracked the decline of snow and ice cover in the Northern Hemisphere, the northward march at high latitudes of vegetation typically found farther south, and other changes that suggest the feedback has kicked in.

This latest study says "yes, the feedback is working as we suspected it would be," says Dr. Serreze, who was not part of the team conducting the research. "But it also argues that maybe the feedback is stronger than we thought it would be."

That last point will likely be challenged, he adds, as part of the scientific process.

"Putting numbers to these feedbacks is a tough thing to do," he says. Still, "this is an important paper. I see this as a significant advance in climate science."

As one of the world's two deep-freeze thermostats, Antarctica is still chiller-in-chief. But because the Arctic is warmer than its southern counterpart, small changes in temperatures at the top of the world have a relatively larger effect on ice and snow cover, researchers say.

Reality Check on Climate Models

Mark Flanner, a climate researcher at the University of Michigan who led the team, says the goal of the new study was to provide a reality check on global climate models' representations of the impact that declining snow and ice has on the Earth's so-called radiation budget. The radiation budget is a kind of bookkeeping process that tries to account for all the sunlight Earth receives and either reflects or converts into heat.

Using satellite measurements as well as field measurements of the extent of snow and ice cover, the team teased out details of seasonal patterns in the amount of solar radiation the Northern Hemisphere's snow and ice reflect.

Snow appears to have its maximum cooling effect—reflecting the most sunlight back into space—in late spring, as the light strengthens but snow cover is still near its maximum extent for the year. Sea ice in the Arctic Ocean has its biggest effect in June, before its annual summer melt-back accelerates, explains Don Perovich, a researcher at the US Army Corps of

Engineers Cold Regions Research and Engineering Laboratory in Hanover, N.H., and a member of the team reporting the results.

That means "it becomes important when you melt snow and ice," he says. "If you start that melting earlier, you tend to have a lower albedo every day throughout the summer," he says. Albedo is a measure of a surface's ability to reflect light.

Research published by a different team in 2009 showed that at least for the Canadian Archipelago, the melt season grew at a rate of about seven days per decade during the 1979–2008 period. Most of that expansion has come at season's end, the team reported, but the onset of the melt season was coming earlier as well.

But the eyebrow-arching moment for Dr. Flanner and his colleagues came in comparing real-world measurements of the ice-snow feedback with those from models.

Twice the Decline in Cooling Effect

According to the team, the measured decline in the cooling effect of the Northern Hemisphere's shrinking cryosphere associated with a 1-degree Celsius increase in Northern Hemisphere temperatures was more than twice that predicted by climate models.

"The reduction was somewhat surprising," Flanner says.

The team acknowledges that the study has its limitations.

For instance, the 30-year period "is right on the edge of being long enough" to separate long-term trends from year-to-year changes in conditions that occur naturally, Flanner says.

But Dr. Perovich adds that many of the assumptions the team had to make as it analyzed the data are likely to prove conservative.

12

Permafrost Is Melting

Ben Cubby

Ben Cubby is the environmental editor for the Sydney Morning Herald *newspaper.*

A 2012 report demonstrates that Arctic permafrost—continually frozen soil, rock, and other material—has reached a tipping point of irreversible melting due to human-induced global warming. This threatens to unlock the vast amounts of carbon in the ice—in the form of ancient forests—and these emissions may total up to 39 percent of all emissions. At the time of the report, the exact rate and scope of melting was not known, but scientists observe that methane leaking from these areas has risen significantly. Experts warn that action must be taken to prevent permafrost melt, as the release of greenhouse gases can be equal to that generated by human activity.

The world is on the cusp of a "tipping point" into dangerous climate change, according to new data gathered by scientists measuring methane leaking from the Arctic permafrost and a report presented to the United Nations on Tuesday [November 27, 2012].

"The permafrost carbon feedback is irreversible on human time scales," says the report, *Policy Implications of Warming Permafrost*. "Overall, these observations indicate that large-scale thawing of permafrost may already have started."

Unlocking a Vast Carbon Tank

While countries the size of Australia tally up their greenhouse emissions in hundreds of millions of tonnes, the Arctic's stores are measured in tens of billions.

Human-induced emissions now appear to have warmed the Arctic enough to unlock this vast carbon bank, with stark implications for international efforts to hold global warming to a safe level. Ancient forests locked under ice tens of thousands of years ago are beginning to melt and rot, releasing vast amounts of greenhouse gases into the air.

The report estimates the greenhouse gases leaking from the thawing Arctic will eventually add more to emissions than last year's [2011's] combined carbon output of the US and Europe—a statistic which means present global plans to hold climate change to an average 2 degree temperature rise this century are now likely to be much more difficult.

Until very recently permafrost was thought to have been melting too slowly to make a meaningful difference to temperatures this century, so it was left out of the Kyoto Protocol, and ignored by many climate change models.

"Permafrost emissions could ultimately account for up to 39 per cent of total emissions," said the report's lead author, Kevin Schaefer, of the University of Colorado, who presented it at climate negotiations in Doha, Qatar. "This must be factored in to treaty negotiations expected to replace the Kyoto Protocol."

Crucial Scientific Field Work

What isn't known is the precise rate and scale of the melt, and that is being tackled in a remarkable NASA experiment that hardly anyone has heard of, but which could prove to be one of the most crucial pieces of scientific field work undertaken this century.

The findings, for now, are still under wraps. "But I think 'tantalising' is probably the right word," said Charles Miller, the principal investigator in NASA's Carbon in Arctic Reservoirs Vulnerability Experiment, or CARVE.

His office is a rugged little Sherpa passenger aircraft, stripped of seating and packed with electronics and sensors. Each day, the plane criss-crosses the ice fields, forests and tundra of Alaska, skimming along at low altitude, hugging the contours of the ground.

What the scientists are searching for is invisible to the human eye—the haze of methane and CO2 that hovers low over the landscape in summer as the permafrost melts.

"I've seen the annual migration of the caribou—thousands of animals in a single line stretching for 10 kilometres along a ridge, led by a bull with giant antlers," Professor Miller said. "There are grizzly bears in the forests, and moose wallowing in lakes—it's just incredibly beautiful up here."

But it isn't the scenery that brought them to Alaska. What the scientists are searching for is invisible to the human eye—the haze of methane and CO2 [carbon dioxide] that hovers low over the landscape in summer as the permafrost melts.

"We fly like a rollercoaster, in a flight line that touches the 'boundary layer' [a layer where the air from the ground mingles with higher altitudes] and then we fly down, and come straight back up. We keep doing that repeatedly," Professor Miller said.

The plane dips in and out of the methane plumes, sucking up data that hints at the extent and speed of the permafrost melt.

"We're finding very, very interesting changes, particularly in terms of methane concentrations," he said. "When scientists say 'interesting', it usually means 'not what we expected'. We're seeing biological activity in various places in Alaska that's much more active than I would have expected, and also much more variable from place to place. . . . There are changes as much as 10 to 12 parts per million for CO2—so that's telling us that the local biology is doing something like five or six years worth of change in the space of a few hundred metres."

Methane is not present in the frozen soil, but is instead created as the earth thaws and organic matter is consumed by tiny organisms.

"If the Arctic becomes warmer and drier, we will see it released as carbon dioxide, but if it is warmer and wetter it will be released as methane."

The findings of the first year of the experiment are so complex that Professor Miller and his team at NASA's Jet Propulsion Laboratory are still trying to work out exactly what they have found. The results are being kept secret, which is standard practice while the numbers are crunched and the work is submitted to a peer-review process.

"What we can say is that methane is significantly elevated in places—about 2000 parts per billion, against a normal background of about 1850 parts per billion," he said. "It's interesting because the models are predicting one thing and what we are observing is something fairly different."

Permafrost Melt Is Underrated

The rate of melt was "deeply concerning", said Andy Pitman, the director of Australia's Centre of Excellence for Climate System Science, an adviser to the Climate Commission, and a lead author of the Intergovernmental Panel on Climate Change's [IPCC] reports.

"It had been assumed that on the timescale of the 21st century, that the effects of methane release would be relatively small compared to other effects—that's why it has been largely left out of the climate models," Professor Pitman said.

"I think it's fair to say that until recently climate scientists underrated the rate at which permafrost melt could release methane. I think we've been shown to be over-conservative. It's happening faster than we had thought. . . . This is not good news."

The report presented to the UN said a tipping point could still be averted if the world moved to cut emissions from fossil fuels fast.

"The target climate for the climate change treaty is not out of date," Professor Schaefer told Fairfax Media. "However, negotiation of anthropogenic emissions targets to meet the 2 degree warming target must account for emissions from thawing permafrost. Otherwise, we risk overshooting the target climate."

Negotiation of anthropogenic emissions targets . . . must account for emissions from thawing permafrost. Otherwise, we risk overshooting the target climate.

The report pointed out that permafrost carbon feedback had not been included in the Fourth IPCC report, the most recent update from the UN's climate body, published in 2007.

"Participating modelling teams have completed their climate projections in support of the Fifth Assessment Report, but these projections do not include the permafrost carbon feedback," the report said. "Consequently, the IPCC Fifth Assessment Report, due for release in stages between September 2013 and October 2014, will not include the potential effects of the permafrost carbon feedback on global climate."

The cost of this omission could be high if measured in financial terms, according to Pep Canadell, a CSIRO [Commonwealth Scientific and Industrial Research Organisation] scientist and executive director of the Global Carbon Project, which tallies how much CO_2 humans can release before the climate can be expected to warm to dangerous levels.

"If you were to take the price of a tonne of carbon to be $23 like Australia does, you are looking at an extra cost of about $35 billion for the permafrost," Dr Canadell said. "That's on top of the hundreds of billions we already know it will cost to slow emissions to reach a 2 degree level. It's a significant problem in the carbon budget."

The evidence that major change is already happening is trickling in not just from the NASA measurements, but from ground-based tests.

"There is compelling evidence, not just that permafrost will thaw, but that it is already rapidly thawing," said Ben Abbott, a researcher at the Institute of Arctic Biology at the University of Alaska, Fairbanks.

"Borehole measurements, where temperature readings are taken at multiple depths within the soil, show more than 2 degree soil warming in some areas of Alaska. While that may not sound like much, a lot of permafrost is at or just below freezing. The difference between minus 1 degree and 1 degree is the difference between a fresh frozen meal and a rotten mess."

Carbon Release More Quick than Models Suggest

In a piece in the journal *Nature*, Mr Abbott and fellow researcher Edward Schuur from the University of Florida summarised recent findings from experts in the field.

About 1700 billion tonnes of organic carbon is held in frozen northern soils, they said—about four times more than all the carbon emitted by human activity in modern times and twice as much as is present in the atmosphere now. The impact of thawing soil on the speed of climate change will be similar to the total rate of logging in all forests around the world, they calculated.

"Our collective estimate is that carbon will be released more quickly than models suggest, and at levels that are cause for serious concern," they wrote. "We calculate that permafrost thaw will release the same order of magnitude of carbon as deforestation if current rates of deforestation continue."

Like Professor Miller, Mr Abbott's job involves long expeditions into the Alaskan tundra.

"I think it's easy for people to feel that the Arctic is just a far away place that will never have any direct effect on their life," he said. "[But] the last time a majority of permafrost carbon was thawed and lost to the atmosphere, temperatures increased by 6 degrees. That's a different world. Too often climate change is depicted as a story of drowning polar bears and third world countries. Human-caused climate change has the potential to change our way of life. Mix in the potent feedbacks from the permafrost system and it becomes clear that we need to act now."

13

Permafrost Warming Is Widely Misunderstood

Guido Grosse et al.

Guido Grosse is a research assistant professor at the University of Alaska, Fairbanks. The other authors of the following viewpoint are Vladimir Romanovsky, Frederick E. Nelson, Jerry Brown, and Antoni G. Lewkowicz. Nelson is a geography professor at the University of Delaware, while Brown is a member of the International Permafrost Association. Lewkowicz is a geography professor at the University of Ottawa, Canada.

Using the term "melting" to describe thawing permafrost promotes misinterpretations of the process. Melting refers to the transition of a solid to a liquid, and permafrost—which contains a variety of materials and may, in fact, be ice-free—does not completely liquefy when warming. It also leads to misinterpretations of its possible impacts; with particles that remain solid, thawing permafrost can be compared to a defrosting frozen dinner, unlike melting glaciers and ice sheets. Consequently, the term oversimplifies the processes of geophysics and carelessly communicates research on permafrost to the public. Science writers, journalists, and editors are highly encouraged to use the correct terminology to avoid these misunderstandings.

As global climate change is becoming an increasingly important political and social issue, it is essential for the cryospheric and global change research communities to speak with a single voice when using basic terminology to communicate research results and describe underlying physical processes. Experienced science communicators have highlighted the importance of using the correct terms to communicate research results to the media and general public. The consequences of scientists using improper terminology are at best oversimplification, but they more likely involve misunderstandings of the facts by the public.

A glaring example of scientifically incorrect terminology appearing frequently in scientific and public communication relates to reports on the degradation of permafrost. Numerous research papers have appeared in recent years, broadly echoed in the news media, describing the "melting of permafrost," its effects in the Arctic, and its feedbacks on climate through the carbon cycle. Although permafrost researchers have attempted to distinguish between the appropriate term "permafrost thawing" and the erroneous "permafrost melting", the latter is still used widely. A Web-based search using the phrase "permafrost melting" reveals hundreds of occurrences, many from highly regarded news and scientific organizations, including Reuters, *New Scientist*, ABC, *The Guardian*, Discovery News, *Smithsonian* magazine, the National Science Foundation, and others.

"Permafrost melting" is partly an oversimplification that ignores basic geophysical processes and partly sloppy science communication.

A Misinterpretation of the Process

"Permafrost melting" is incorrect terminology that results from a misinterpretation of the physical process of permafrost degradation. "Melting" describes a physical phase change during a temperature increase when a solid substance is transformed into a liquid state. Hence, the term "permafrost melting" suggests the transition of solidly frozen permafrost terrain into a liquid. However, permafrost is properly defined as "all ground (earth material) that remains below 0° Celsius for at least two consecutive years." As such, it is composed of soils, sediments, bedrock, and organic materials, which may or may not include water in the form of ice. Some of these substrates contain ice in pore space and cracks, or include larger bodies of almost pure ice, while others are completely ice-free. Ice-rich permafrost, like the Siberian Yedoma-type deposits, contains more than 70% ice by volume in its upper 30 meters. Warming this ground above 0°C will have dramatic effects on the terrain due to the volume loss from melting ice and subsequent differential subsidence of the land surface, a process often referred to as thermokarst. But even in such ice-rich permafrost types, only that 70% or so of the ground volume constituting the ice melts—not the mineral and organic component of the permafrost. To speak of "melting permafrost" implies that all components of permafrost are turning into a liquid, which is erroneous. In terrain types with much less ground ice, which are widespread in the Arctic and in alpine mountain regions, warming above 0°C will have virtually no direct impact on the land surface.

A Misinterpretation of the Potential Consequences

Use of the term "permafrost melting" not only indicates misunderstanding of permafrost properties and the processes involved in permafrost degradation, but also leads to misinterpretation of the potential consequences of this process. Because melting of ice—a physically valid phrase—is common knowledge, the inappropriate phrase "permafrost melting" conveys an image of permafrost as a form of underground ice, undergoing a complete solid-to-liquid transition much like glaciers and ice sheets. Defrosting food is a much better analogy for communicating about permafrost thaw to the general public. Like most foodstuffs, permafrost does not liquefy completely when its temperature exceeds 0°C. Similarly, during permafrost thaw, only the ground ice melts, while mineral and organic particles, which represent the majority in many permafrost types by volume, remain solid.

Although some individuals may regard "permafrost melting" as an acceptable simplification, we advocate a different view. "Permafrost melting" is partly an oversimplification that ignores basic geophysical processes and partly sloppy science communication, both with unwanted implications for communicating scientific information and educating students and the public about climate change.

This example from permafrost research has equivalents in other geophysical research fields—for example, some writers refer to sea ice on the Arctic Ocean as an "ice cap," although that term properly applies to bodies of glacial ice of particular dimensions and morphology. Sometimes scientific writers unknowingly neglect or oversimplify basic physical, biological, or chemical processes, especially when working across disciplines. We strongly encourage authors working on cross-disciplinary topics or reaching outside their own research fields to ensure that they use basic terminology accurately. We also encourage reviewers and editors of scientific journals receiving manuscripts to be more rigorous in following up on the use of appropriate scientific terminology for basic physical processes.

Organizations to Contact

The editors have compiled the following list of organizations concerned with the issues debated in this book. The descriptions are derived from materials provided by the organizations. All have publications or information available for interested readers. The list was compiled on the date of publication of the present volume; the information provided here may change. Be aware that many organizations take several weeks or longer to respond to inquiries, so allow as much time as possible.

Antarctic and Southern Ocean Coalition (ASOC)
1630 Connecticut Ave. NW, 3rd Floor, Washington, DC   20009
(202) 234-2480 • fax: (202) 387-4823
e-mail: secretariat@asoc.org
website: www.asoc.org

Founded in 1978, the Antarctic and Southern Ocean Coalition (ASOC) is the only nongovernmental organization (NGO) working full time to preserve the Antarctic continent and its surrounding Southern Ocean. A coalition of over thirty NGOs interested in Antarctic environmental protection, ASOC represents the environmental community at Antarctic governance meetings and works to promote important Antarctic conservation goals. Its website offers information on how climate change affects the region.

Cato Institute
1000 Massachusetts Ave. NW, Washington, DC   20001-5403
(202) 842-0200 • fax: (202) 842-3490
website: www.cato.org

The Cato Institute is an organization dedicated to espousing the libertarian principles of free market economics and limited government intervention in all areas of life. As such, Cato promotes energy and environmental policy that discourages government policies and incentives to push the development of sustainable energy sources, instead advocating for the free market's ability to provide the best solutions to environmental issues such as global warming. The Institute worries that government intervention to protect the environment will only stifle economic liberty. Current articles and commentary by Cato concerning glacier and ice melt include "History to Repeat: Greenland's Ice to Survive, United Nations to Continue Holiday Party" and "The Current Wisdom: Throwing Science Overboard to Get a Sea-Level Disaster." These and other articles are available on its website.

Center for American Progress (CAP)

1333 H St. NW, 10th Floor, Washington, DC   20005
(202) 682-1611
website: www.americanprogress.org

Center for American Progress (CAP) is a progressive public policy institute that seeks to promote liberal values and point out the flaws of conservative government while encouraging the media to honestly present, analyze, and critique important current issues. CAP advocates for government policy that protects the environment by encouraging the development of sustainable energy technologies and that reduces global dependence on carbon producing energy sources. Print and multimedia publications on these issues, including "Climate Change, Migration, and Conflict" and "Certainty on the Science of Climate Change," can be accessed on CAP's website.

Center for Climate and Energy Solutions (C2ES)

2101 Wilson Blvd., Suite 550, Arlington, VA   22201
(703) 516-4146 • fax: (703) 516-9551
website: www.c2es.org

The Center for Climate and Energy Solutions (C2ES) is an independent, nonpartisan, nonprofit organization working to advance policy and action to address the twin challenges of energy and climate change. Launched in November 2011, C2ES is the successor to the Pew Center on Global Climate Change; its founder, Eileen Claussen, and its senior team continue to lead the effort. The Center provides online articles addressing glacier and ice melt, including "Climate Change at Kili" and "Fast Action to Reduce the Risks of Climate Change: US Options to Limit Short-Lived Climate Pollutants."

Center for the Study of Carbon Dioxide and Global Change
PO Box 25697, Tempe, AZ 85285-5697
(480) 966-3719
website: www.co2science.org

The Center for the Study of Carbon Dioxide and Global Change seeks to be a voice of scientific reason to counter what it dubs "alarmist global warming propaganda." The Center provides scientific analysis of the rising levels of atmospheric carbon dioxide (CO_2) in its weekly online magazine, *CO_2 Science*. Additionally, the organization posts online instructions for experiments that individuals can conduct in the classroom or at home to personally assess CO_2 enrichment and depletion.

Climate Institute
900 17th St. NW, Suite 700, Washington, DC 20006
(202) 552-4723 • fax: (202) 737-6410
e-mail: info@climate.org
website: www.climate.org

The Climate Institute is a nonprofit organization with the goals of identifying methods of reducing environmentally harmful emissions and informing both the public and policy makers about current options to halt global climate change. The organization attempts to maintain a reliable, unbiased source of information on global warming. Specific topics addressed by the Institute with regard to climate change include sea level rise, water, and glacier and ice melt. Publications on these issues and others can be found on its website.

Earth Policy Institute (EPI)
1350 Connecticut Ave. NW, Suite 403, Washington, DC 20036
(202) 496-9290 • fax: (202) 496-9325

e-mail: epi@earthpolicy.org
website: www.earthpolicy.org

Since its founding in 2001, Earth Policy Institute (EPI) has sought to inform individuals worldwide about the problems presented by glacier and ice melt and to provide viable solutions for a sustainable future. EPI employs the Internet, mass communications media, and book publication to get its message out to the public. Many of the organization's publications and documents are available online.

GlacierWorks

e-mail: info@glacierworks.org
website: www.glacierworks.org

Founded by mountaineer, photographer, and filmmaker David Breashears, GlacierWorks is a nonprofit organization that illustrates the changes to Himalayan glaciers through art, science, and adventure. Since 2007, GlacierWorks has undertaken ten expeditions to document the current state of the glaciers, retracing the steps of pioneering mountain photographers in order to capture new images that precisely match the early photographic records. Its team uses specially designed hardware and software to capture the images in detail, which are available on its website.

National Aeronautics and Space Administration (NASA) Cryospheric Sciences Program

NASA Headquarters, Suite 2R40, Washington, DC   20546-000
(202) 358-0001 • fax: (202) 358-4338
website: http://ice.nasa.gov

Established by President Dwight D. Eisenhower in 1958, NASA formed from the National Advisory Committee on Aeronautics (NACA), which had been researching flight technology for more than forty years. Known for its space research and exploration, NASA also provides information on sea ice, ice caps and glaciers, ice shelves, snow, river and lake ice, and permafrost through its Cryospheric Sciences Program. On its website, the program offers data from NASA satellites and other instruments that monitor the earth's cryosphere.

National Snow & Ice Data Center (NSIDC)

CIRES, 449 UCB, University of Colorado
Boulder, CO   80309-0449
(303) 492-6199 • fax: (303) 492-2468
e-mail: nsidc@nsidc.org
website: http://nsidc.org

The National Snow & Ice Data Center (NSIDC) supports research into the world's frozen realms: the snow, ice, glaciers, frozen ground, and climate interactions that make up Earth's cryosphere. The Center manages and distributes scientific data, creates tools for data access, supports data users, performs scientific research, and educates the public about the cryosphere. In addition, NSIDC distributes more than five hundred cryospheric data sets for researchers, from both satellite and ground observations, which is available online. The Center also maintains a section on glaciers on its website, World Glacier Inventory Documentation.

US Environmental Protection Agency (EPA)

Ariel Rios Building, 1200 Pennsylvania Ave. NW
Washington, DC   20460
(202) 272-0167
website: www.epa.gov

The US Environmental Protection Agency (EPA) is the federal government agency charged with protecting the environment and the health of American citizens through the development and enforcement of environmental regulations, grant giving, conducting research and publishing studies, and working in partnership with nongovernmental organizations. Additionally, the agency seeks to educate the public about current environmental issues. On its website, the EPA provides the latest information on topics related to climate change and the world's glaciers and ice sheets.

US Geological Survey (USGS)

USGS National Center, 12201 Sunrise Valley Dr.
Reston, VA   20192

(703) 648-5953
website: www.usgs.gov

The US Geological Survey (USGS) is a science organization that provides impartial information on the health of ecosystems and environment, the natural hazards that pose threats, the natural resources that are relied upon, the impacts of climate and land-use change, and the core science systems that provide timely, relevant, and useable information. Its website offers information and publications on glaciers, ice, and other parts of the cryosphere.

US Permafrost Association (USPA)
PO Box 750141, Fairbanks, AK 99775-0141
(302) 831-0852 • fax: (302) 831-6654
e-mail: info@uspermafrost.org
website: www.uspermafrost.org

The purpose of the US Permafrost Association (USPA) is to encourage scientific and engineering investigations in permafrost and related topics and to disseminate results related to permafrost research, sharing of knowledge and data in permafrost science, and awareness of permafrost among the public, as well as training of new generations of scientists and engineers to work in fields related to permafrost science and engineering. Reports, publications, and archives of the *IPA New Bulletin* are available on its website.

World Glacier Monitoring Service (WGMS)
Department of Geography, University of Zurich
Winterthurerstrasse 190, Zurich CH-8057
   Switzerland
+41 44 635 5139 • fax: +41 44 635 6841
e-mail: wgms@geo.uzh.ch
website: www.geo.uzh.ch/microsite/wgms/index.html

The University of Zurich's World Glacier Monitoring Service (WGMS) collects standardized observations on changes in mass, volume, area, and length of glaciers with time (glacier fluctuations), as well as statistical information on the distribution of perennial surface ice in space (glacier inventories). On-line, WGMS offers this data, the World Glacier Inventory, and scientific literature from workshops and conferences on glacier monitoring and studies. It also maintains the WGMS Library, with more than 220 publications covering glaciology.

Bibliography

Books

Harold Ambler   *Don't Sell Your Coat: Surprising Truths About Climate Change.* East Greenwich, RI: Lansing International Books, 2011.

David Archer and   *The Climate Crisis: An Introductory*
Stefan Rahmstorf   *Guide to Climate Change.* New York: Cambridge University Press, 2010.

Roger G. Barry   *The Global Cryosphere: Past, Present,*
and Thian Yew   *and Future.* New York: Cambridge
Gan   University Press, 2011.

Robert M. Carter   *Climate, the Counter Consensus: A Palaeoclimatologist Speaks.* London: Stacey International, 2010.

Philip Conkling   *The Fate of Greenland: Lessons from*
et al.   *Abrupt Climate Change.* Cambridge, MA: MIT Press, 2011.

Mark Lynas   *Six Degrees: Our Future on a Hotter Planet.* Washington, DC: National Geographic, 2008.

Shawn J. Marshall   *The Cryosphere.* Princeton, NJ: Princeton University Press, 2012.

Patrick J.   *Climate of Extremes: Global Warming*
Michaels and   *Science They Don't Want You to*
Robert C. Balling   *Know.* Washington, DC: Cato
Jr.   Institute, 2009.

A.W. Montford — *The Hockey Stick Illusion: Climategate and the Corruption of Science.* London: Stacey International, 2010.

Henry Pollack — *A World Without Ice.* New York: Avery, 2010.

Roy W. Spencer — *The Great Global Warming Blunder: How Mother Nature Fooled the World's Top Climate Scientists.* New York: Encounter Books, 2010.

Gabrielle Walker — *Antarctica: An Intimate Portrait of the World's Most Mysterious Continent.* New York: Bloomsbury, 2012.

Peter D. Ward — *The Flooded Earth: Our Future in a World Without Ice Caps.* New York: Basic Books, 2010.

Periodicals and Internet Sources

Larry Bell — "Goodness Glaciers! More Unprecedented Global Warming Meltdowns?" *Forbes*, August 4, 2012.

John Carey — "Global Warming: Faster than Expected?" *Scientific American*, November 2012.

Ed Douglas — "How to Grow a Glacier," *New Scientist*, February 2, 2008.

Barbara Fraser — "Melting in the Andes: Goodbye Glaciers," *Nature*, November 7, 2012.

Justin Gillis — "As Permafrost Thaws, Scientists Study the Risks," *New York Times*, December 16, 2011.

Mary Beth Griggs   "How Do We Know How Much Glaciers Are Shrinking?" *Popular Science*, June 28, 2012.

Doug L. Hoffman   "Ice-Shelf Collapse Not Caused by Global Warming," *Resilient Earth*, November 8, 2011.

Aron Lamm   "Polar Ice Is Melting . . . Or Is It?" *Epoch Times*, October 8, 2012.

Michael D. Lemonick   "Nearing a Tipping Point on Melting Permafrost?" Climate Central, February 21, 2013. www.climatecentral.org.

Bill McKibben   "The Arctic Ice Crisis," *Rolling Stone*, August 30, 2012.

New Internationalist   "When the Ice Melts: What's in Store as the World's Coldest Dwelling Place Heats Up?" July–August 2009.

Alissa Opar   "Thawing Permafrost in the Arctic Will Speed Up Global Warming," *Audubon Magazine*, May–June 2010.

Brand Plumer   "Permafrost Thaw—Just How Scary Is It?" *Washington Post*, December 19, 2011.

Patima Prandy and G. Venkatamaran   "Climate Change Effect on Glacier Behavior: A Case Study from the Himalayas," *Earthzine*, February 22, 2012.

Christoph Seidler   "A Costly Mistake: UN Climate
Experts Under Fire for Glacier Melt
Error," *Spiegel Online International*,
January 20, 2010. www.spiegel.de
/international.

Alexandra Witze   "Ice in Motion: As Frozen Lands
Disintegrate, Researchers Rush to
Catch the Collapse," *Science News*,
March 26, 2011.

Index

A

Abbott, Ben, 91–92
Abdalati, Waleed, 14
Albedo effect, 40, 63, 85
Allison, Ian, 26–27
The Alps, 12
American Colorado Plateau, 72
Amundsen Sea, 16
The Andes, 12
Annan, Kofi, 47
Antarctica
    calving glaciers in, 8
    glacier growth in, 26–27
    ice melt in, 54
    ice sheets covering, 12, 14, 16
    melting of, 71–75
    no ice melt in, 76–81
    overview, 71–72, 76–77
    permafrost in, 8
    sea level rise around, 64, 72–73
    snow cover in, 9
Antarctic Peninsula area, 26–27
Appenzeller, Tim, 10–21
Arctic
    higher sensitivity of, 40–41
    ice melt, 59–61
    ice melt, exaggerated, 47
    ice melt, irreversible, 36–42
    permafrost in, 8
Arctic Institute Centre, 45
Arctic Oscillation, 41
Argentina, 11, 26
Asia, 32, 33
Atlantic multidecadal oscillation (AMO), 62–63

Australia, 87, 91
Australian Antarctic Division, 26
Australia's Centre of Excellence for Climate System Science, 89

B

Bindschadler, Robert, 17–18, 74–75
Black carbon. *See* Stove soot
Mt. Blanc, 26
Bolivia, 12, 18
Bolivian Ministry of Planning and Development, 20
Brandon, Mark, 45, 46–48, 51
Brigstocke, Marcus, 45
British Antarctic Survey, 27, 78
Brown, Gordon, 47–48
Brown, Jerry, 9

C

California Institution of Technology, 43
Calving of glaciers, 8, 68
Canada, 8, 26
Canadell, Pep, 90–91
Canadian Archipelago, 85
Canadian High Arctic, 41
Carbon dioxide emissions
    ice melt and, 38
    impact of, 77
    permafrost and, 87, 88, 91–92
    as pollution, 65
    stove soot, 31–35